D1809828

# Vegetarian Visitor 2008

# Vegetarian Visitor 2008

**Edited by Annemarie Weitzel**

Jon Carpenter

to Shetlands

This edition first published 2008 by
Jon Carpenter Publishing, Alder House, Market Street, Charlbury, Oxfordshire OX7 3PH
Tel and fax: 01608 811969  E-mail: vv@joncarpenter.co.uk
This compilation © Annemarie Weitzel
Whilst the publishers must disclaim responsibility for any inaccuracy, the information in
this guide has been carefully checked at the time of going to press
ISBN  978-1-906067-00-7
Printed and bound by Antony Rowe Ltd, Chippenham

# Contents

# How to use this guide

Welcome to the new edition of *Vegetarian Visitor*, listing private houses, guest houses, hotels, cafés, restaurants and pubs which take catering for vegetarians and vegans seriously. All establishments in the guide have been supplied with a 'We're in Vegetarian Visitor 2008' sticker, to make them easily recognisable.

## Activity holidays, Special breaks, Courses

Entries are listed alphabetically by county, then name. Almost all offer bed and breakfast: 'see also page XX' tells you where to find further details, including websites and email addresses.

## Accommodation and Eateries

Entries are grouped geographically in sections and within each section alphabetically by county, then town or village, then name. London is divided into Central, East, North, South and West and entries are arranged first by postcode, then alphabetically by name.

Accommodation addresses have coded information as well as a general description. The codes indicate the following:

| | | | | | |
|---|---|---|---|---|---|
| **H** | Hotel | **G** | Guest House | **PH** | Private house |

**INS**   Inspected under one of the schemes operating in Britain; full details can be obtained from the establishment concerned if required

**L**   Licensed

**DA**   Disabled access

**V**   Exclusively vegetarian: entries without this code also cater for non-vegetarians

**Ve**   Also catering for vegans; please mention you are a vegan when you contact the establishment

**Vegan**   Exclusively vegan

**NS**   No smoking anywhere on the premises (may include garden)

**pNS**   Smoking restricted to certain areas only

**CN**   Car necessary: a car/taxi journey or extended walk is needed from the nearest public transport

**Acc2**   Accommodation for two adults; children travelling with their parents can sometimes be accommodated additionally

Price categories for bed and breakfast per person per night (minimum, guide only):

**CatA** over £30; **CatB** £20-£30; **CatC** under £20.

Many cafés, restaurants and pubs have a short description, as well as coded information. Opening times may vary not only by establishment but also by season. As a general rule, cafés will be open during the day but not in the evening, and are often closed on Sundays and Bank Holidays. Restaurants are generally open for lunch and in the evening; they may be closed one day a week, but this is not usually Sunday. Pubs are normally open seven days a week and may be open all day and in the evening. If you want to be sure that your chosen eating place is open, please give them a ring. The codes give the following information:

| | | | | | |
|---|---|---|---|---|---|
| **R** | Restaurant | **C** | Café | **P** | Pub |

| | |
|---|---|
| **L** | Licensed |
| **a** | A selection of vegetarian dishes daily, as well as non-vegetarian food; quite often at least one vegan dish is also on the menu |
| **b** | Vegetarian food only |
| **c** | Vegetarian and vegan food only |
| **d** | Vegan food only |
| **w** | Wholefood |
| **org** | Organic produce used when possible |

The **NS** and **pNS** codes have been deleted, as all premises are smoke-free. England, Wales and Scotland now have a ban on smoking in public places, which includes restaurants, cafés and pubs.

I would be delighted to hear from any user of this guide. If you have stayed or eaten somewhere not listed, please drop me a line with the name and address and I will contact them for next year's edition.

Annemarie Weitzel
2 Home Farm Cottages, Sandy Lane, St Paul's Cray, Kent BR5 3HZ
e-mail: annemarie@weitzel.freeserve.co.uk

# Activity Holidays, Special Breaks, Courses

## England

## Hazel Bank Country House

☎017687 77248, fax 017687 77373

**Rosthwaite, Borrowdale, Keswick, Cumbria CA12 5XB**

Please contact us for details of the watercolour painting courses we run in July. See also page 69.

## Nab Cottage

☎ 015394 35311, fax 015394 35493

**Rydal, Ambleside, Cumbria LA22 9SD**

Retreat breaks, workshops and courses in yoga, dance, massage, transforming cellular memory. The workshop/venue space in the attached barn is ideal for groups, yoga, dance, walking, celebrations. See also page 70.

## Rothay Manor

☎ 015394 33605, fax 015394 33607

**Rothay Bridge, Ambleside, Cumbria LA22 0EH**

We offer the following types of specialised holidays: painting, music, gardening, antiques, bridge, walking, Lake District heritage. See also page 67.

## Devon Valley Retreat

☎ 01548 821180

**Lower Norris House, South Brent, nr Totnes, Devon TQ10 9NJ**

Feeling stressed?? Unwind in beautiful, hidden Devon valley. Aromatherapy massage, reflexology and spiritual healing available. Healing, painting and other courses held occasionally. Groups welcome. See also page 34.

# Tor Cottage

☎ 01822 860248, fax 01822 860126

**Chillaton, Devon PL16 0JE**

We are a Romantic Retreat and a special place for Birthdays, Anniversaries and Honeymoons. Special Autumn-Spring Breaks available, offering one night free of charge, or 10% discount on a 7-night holiday throughout the year. No children. No smoking. No pets. See also page 31.

# Polemonium Plantery

☎ 01429 881529

**28 Sunnyside, Trimdon Grange, Trimdon Station, Durham TS29 6HF**

We offer Vegetarian Cookery, Green Family Activity and Cycling/Walking weekends. See also page 59.

# Cheltenham Lawn

☎ and fax 01242 526638

**5 Pittville Lawn, Cheltenham, Gloucestershire GL52 2BE**

We run art/design drawing workshops and textile and printmaking courses. See also page 52.

# Claridge House

☎ 01342 832150, fax 01342 836730

**Dormans Road, Dormansland, Lingfield, Surrey RH7 6QH**

Claridge House runs courses in yoga, reiki, circle dancing, poetry and personal development. See also page 22

# Bishops Wood Environmental Education Centre

☎ 01299 250513

**Crossway Green. Stourport-on-Severn, Worcestershire DY13 9SE**

This unique centre is one of the best examples of environmental design and construction techniques in the country and attracts visitors from far and wide. It provides courses ranging from willow sculpture to environmental management for industry and from woodland survival crafts to reed-bed treatment of sewage! For further information please contact the Head of Centre at the above address.

Accommodation can be found at Tytchney Gables, just 1½ miles away, and Mrs Margaret Peters can also provide information about activities at the Centre and about the Friends of Bishops Wood group. See page 57.

# **Wales**

## Heartspring      ☎ 01267 241999
### Hill House, Llansteffan, nr Carmarthen, Carmarthenshire SA33 5JG

We run healing and therapeutic residential retreats by the sea, with a choice of complementary therapies and delicious organic vegetarian food. We also have vegetarian self-catering apartments for peaceful holidays. See also page 85.

## Glanhelyg      ☎ 01239 682119/682482
### Llechryd, Cardigan, Ceredigion SA43 2NJ

Painting courses run by visiting tutors are sometimes available. See also page 86.

## Awen Vegetarian B&B      ☎ 01495 244615
### Penrhiwgwair Cottage, Twyn Road, Abercarn, Newport, Gwent NP11 5AS

Please ask about our courses in Reiki I, II and III. See also page 84.

## Cuffern Manor      ☎ 01437 710071
### Roch, Haverfordwest, Pembrokeshire SA62 6HB

Please contact us for details of our complementary health and arts courses. See also page 86.

## Elan Valley Hotel  ☎ 01597 810448, fax 01597 810824
### Elan Valley, Rhayader, Powys LD6 5HN

We organise wild mushroom foraging, bird watching, watercolour landscapes and life drawing special breaks with expert tutors. See also page 82.

## Trericket Mill Vegetarian Guesthouse
☎ 01982 560312, fax 01982 560768
### Erwood, Builth Wells, Powys LD2 3TQ

Host of Bicycle Beano vegetarian cycling holidays. Please contact us for details. See also page 81.

# Scotland

## Drumskeoch Farm B&B  ☎ 01465 841172
### Pinwherry, nr Girvan, Ayrshire KA26 0QB

Courses in herbal medicine, willow workshops and other sustainable rural crafts run by local and visiting tutors. See also page 90.

## Woodland  ☎ 01549 441715
### Rosehall, by Lairg, Sutherland IV27 4BD

We offer yoga retreats, guided walks and wildlife weekends. Also bicycle hire. See also page 98.

# London

## Central London

### Lincoln House Hotel

☎ 020 7486 7630, fax 020 7486 0166

**33 Gloucester Place, London W1U 8HY**

e-mail: reservations@lincoln-house-hotel.co.uk
website: www.lincoln-house-hotel.co.uk

See display ad below.
H INS CatB Ve pNS Acc50

*Cafés, restaurants, pubs*

**Carnevale Restaurant** ☎ 020 7250 3452
135 Whitecross Street, London EC1Y 8JL       R L c org

**Tas Restaurant** ☎ 020 7430 9721/9722
37 Farringdon Road, London EC1M 3JB          R L a org
**Zen Garden** ☎ 020 7242 6128
88 Leather Lane, London EC1N 7TT          R L b
**The Place Below** ☎ 020 7329 0789
St. Mary-le-Bow Church, Cheapside, London EC2V 6AU          C a
**Beatroot** ☎ 020 7437 8591
92 Berwick Street, Soho, London W1V 3PP
A budget healthy vegetarian feast at Beatroot. Tofu stir-fry, Jamaican
curry, home-baked quiche, seasonal salads. Fresh superfood
smoothies, delicious cakes.          C c
**Chai Pani** ☎ 020 7258 2000
64 Seymour Street, London W1H 5BW          R L c
**Eat and Two Veg** ☎ 020 7258 8595
50 Marylebone High Street, London W1U 5HN
World's first meat-free diner, open all day. Serving breakfast, lunch
and dinner plus everything in between.          R L c
**La Porte des Indes** ☎ 020 7224 0055
32 Bryanston Street, Marble Arch, London W1H 7EG          R L a
**Mildreds** ☎ 020 7494 1634
45 Lexington Street, Soho, London W1F 9AN          R L c
**Gaby's Deli** ☎ 020 7836 4233
30 Charing Cross Road, London WC2H 0DE          R L a
**World Food Café** ☎ 020 7379 0298
1st Floor, 14 Neal's Yard, Covent Garden, London WC2H 9DP          C c w

# *East London*

## *Cafés, restaurants, pubs*
**Wild Cherry** ☎ 020 8980 6678
241-245 Globe Road, London E2 0JD
See display ad on page 15.          R c
**Pogo Café** ☎ 020 8533 1214
76A Clarence Road, London E5 8HB          R/C d org
**Mulberry Tea Rooms** ☎ 020 8856 3951
Charlton house, Charlton Road, Charlton, London SE7 8RE          C a

# *North London*

## *Cafés, restaurants, pubs*

**Jai Krishna Vegetarian Restaurant** ☎ 020 7272 1680
   161 Stroud Green Road, Finsbury Park, London N4 3PZ      R c
**Rasa N16** ☎ 020 7249 0344
   55 Stoke Newington Church Street, London N16 0AR      R L b
**Café Seventy Nine** ☎ 020 7586 8012
   79 Regents Park Road, London NW1 8UY      C b w org
**Green Note** ☎ 020 7485 9899
   106 Parkway, London NW1 7AN      R/C L c

# South London

## bbputney.com ☎ 020 8785 7609, fax 020 8789 5584
### One Fanthorpe Street, Putney, London SW15 1DZ

e-mail: bbputney@btinternet.com
website: www.bbputney.com

Pip and Robert Taylor look forward to welcoming you to our family home in Putney. We offer a unique English experience in London. Our rooms are comfortable and reasonably priced. There is easy access to Central London and good transport facilities are close by.
PH CatA Ve NS Acc4

### *Cafés, restaurants, pubs*

**Tas Pide** ☎ 020 7928 3300/020 7633 9777
   20-22 New Globe Walk, London SE1 9DR       R L a
**Tas Restaurant** ☎ 020 7403 7200
   72 Borough High Street, London SE1 1XF       R L a
**Domali Café** ☎ 020 8768 0096
   38 Westow Street, Crystal Palace, London SE19 3AH       C L a
**Shahee Bhelpoori** ☎ 020 8679 6275
   1547 London Road, Norbury, London SW16 4AD       R L c

# West London

## Temple Lodge

☎020 8748 8388, tel/fax 020 8748 8322

### 51 Queen Caroline Street, Hammersmith, London W6 9QL

e-mail: templelodgeclub@btconnect.com

Visitors are invited to share the tranquillity of this large Georgian House, described as a peaceful haven, formerly home to the artist Sir Frank Brangwyn. The dining room, where a hearty continental breakfast may be enjoyed, and the sitting room/library look out over a large secluded garden. The bedrooms, with a Scandinavian touch, each have washbasins, with the bathrooms nearby. The West End, Richmond and Kew are very accessible by bus and tube.

G INS CatA V Ve NS Acc18

## Cafés, restaurants, pubs

**The Gate Vegetarian Restaurant** ☎ 020 8748 6932
51 Queen Caroline Street, Hammersmith, London W6 9QL  R L c org
**222 Veggie Vegan Restaurant** ☎ 020 7381 2322
222 North End Road, London W14 9NU                      R L d w org
**Hollyhock Café** ☎ 020 8948 6555
Terrace Gardens, Richmond Riverside, Richmond TW10 6UX
Beautiful little café with verandah overlooking Thames in Victorian flower garden. Salads, pastries, soups, ices and chilled drinks served all day.                                                              C c
**Tide Tables** ☎ 020 8948 8285
Riverside, Richmond TW9 1TH
Wonderful setting on banks of River Thames at Richmond. Delicious salads, bakes and snacks, smoothies, ice cream and gourmet coffees and teas served all day.                                    R/C c org

# *Middlesex*

## Cafés, restaurants, pubs

**Pradip's Vegetarian Restaurant** ☎ 020 8909 2232
156 Kenton Road, Harrow HA3 8AZ
Authentic Indian vegetarian cuisine. Enjoy Thali, complete meal from £4.90. Weekend buffet with unlimited selected starters, main course, soft drink.                                                            R c
**Pallavi South Indian Restaurant** ☎ 020 8892 2345
Unit 3, Cross Deep Court, Heath Road, Twickenham TW1 4QJ   R L a

# South and South East

## Dorset (East)

### Glenvale ☎ 01202 553769
**14 Gardens View, East Cliff, Bournemouth BH1 3QA**

website: www.glenvale-vege.co.uk

See display ad above.
G CatB V Ve NS Acc7

### Cowden House ☎ 01300 341377
**Frys Lane, Godmanstone, Dorchester DT2 7AG**

website: www.cowdenhouse.co.uk

A spacious house on the edge of a little village, with beautiful views and surrounded by rolling downland. We provide a peaceful environment with comfort, personal attention and the highest quality vegetarian food, using local organic produce wherever possible.

PH CatB V Ve NS Acc6

## Cafés, restaurants, pubs

**The Salad Centre** ☎ 01202 393673
  667 Christchurch Road, Bournemouth BH7 6AA         C c w org
**Wessex Tales Vegetarian Restaurant** ☎ 01202 309869
  Tudor Corner House, 20 Ashley Road, Boscombe, Bournemouth
  BH1 4LH         R L c w org

# *Hampshire*

# The Barn Vegetarian Guest House

☎ 023 8029 2531

## 112 Lyndhurst Road, Ashurst SO40 7AU

e-mail: info@veggiebarn.net
website: www.veggiebarn.net

Come and enjoy the beauty of the New Forest while staying with people who really know how to look after vegans and vegetarians. 'The Barn' is perfect for walking, cycling and exploring this unique area of England.
G CatB Vegan NS Acc4

## Cafés, restaurants, pubs

**The White Horse** ☎ 01489 892532
  Beeches Hill, Bishops Waltham SO32 1FD         P L a
**Red Mango** ☎ 023 9248 0113
  Havant Arts Centre, East Street, Havant PO9 1BS       C/Bar L a

## Brambles
☎ 01983 862507

**10 Clarence Road, Shanklin PO37 7BH**

e-mail: vegan.brambles@virgin.net
website: www.bramblesvegan.co.uk

See display ad below.
G CatB Vegan NS Acc14

### *Cafés, restaurants, pubs*

**The Cameron Tea Rooms** ☎ 01983 756814
  Dimbola Lodge, Terrace Lane, Freshwater Bay PO40 9QE      C a
**Quay Arts** ☎ 01983 822490
  Sea Street, Newport PO30 5DB      C L a w

# Kent

## Copperfields Vegetarian Guest House

☎ 01843 601247

### 11 Queens Road, Broadstairs CT10 1NU

e-mail: copperfieldsbb@btinternet.com
website: www.copperfieldsbb.co.uk

Award-winning 4 Star Silver Guest House, in picturesque Broadstairs. Our 3 beautiful en-suite rooms have been elegantly furnished with your every need provided for. Copperfields is in the town centre minutes from the beautiful sandy beaches and quaint harbour.
G INS CatB V Ve NS Acc6

### *Cafés, restaurants, pubs*

**Café Mauresque** ☎ 01227 464300
8 Butchery Lane, Canterbury CT1 2JR      R L a
**The Good Food Café** ☎ 01227 456654
Above Canterbury Wholefoods, 1-2 Jewry Lane, Canterbury CT1 2RP
Vegan and gluten-free dishes always available. Organic/biodynamic and Fairtrade where possible. Fabulous gifts and crafts also sold.
Regular art exhibitions.      C c org
**The India Restaurant** ☎ 01303 259155
1 The Old High Street, Folkestone CT20 1RJ
Authentic traditional Indian home cooking. Freshly cooked, grease-free and prepared to order.      R L a
**What The DickInns Public House** ☎ 01634 409912
1 Ross Street, Rochester ME1 2DF
See display ad on page 23.      P L a org
**Brockhill Café at Brockhill Country Park** ☎ 07798 752555
Sandling Road, Saltwood, nr Hythe CT21 4HL
Junction 11 off M20. Children's play area, a beautiful lake, walks and savoury food at savery prices. We are open 10.30-5.30 April to October, 10.30-4 November to March, closed 22 December-4 January.
     C c

# *Surrey*

## Claridge House    ☎ 01342 832150, fax 01342 836730
### Dormans Road, Dormansland, Lingfield RH7 6QH

e-mail: welcome@claridgehouse.quaker.eu.org
website: www.claridgehouse.quaker.eu.org

Claridge House, a warm, peaceful environment offering weekend and midweek courses with a healing focus. Additionally we offer 4-night midweek breaks from £160, full board. Special diets catered for, no single person supplements. Disabled facilities. Open all year including Christmas. See also page 10.

G CatA DA V Ve NS Acc20

## *Cafés, restaurants, pubs*
### Riverside Vegetaria ☎ 020 8546 7992/0609
64 High Street, Kingston upon Thames KT1 1HN       R L c org

*For restaurants in Richmond, Surrey, please see under West London on page 17.*

# WHAT THE DickInns

Feel confident the food served here really *is* vegetarian. Brenda, joint proprietor and strict vegetarian, prepares the food herself and also provides a limited menu for your carnivore friends! Wheelchair friendly and only 4 minutes from Rochester High Street with an attractive garden for eating al fresco with a glass of organic wine on those balmy evenings.

For further information contact Brenda or Graham on ~ 01634 409912 ~ "What the DickInns Bar", Ross Street, Off Delce Road, Rochester, Kent ME₁ 2DF

# Jeake's House

Beautiful listed building dating from 1689, in mediaeval cobblestoned street. Traditional or vegetarian breakfast served in 18th-century galleried former chapel.

Oak-beamed and panelled bedrooms, with brass, mahogany or four-poster beds. En-suite bathrooms, hot drinks trays, televisions. Four-poster honeymoon suite and family room available.

Own private car park, £3.00 per day.

*VisitBritain* 5 Star Gold Award
*Les Routiers* Bed and Breakfast of the Year
*Oldie Magazine* Best Breakfast Award
*Good Hotel Guide* César Award

Tel 01797 222828
Fax 01797 222623
jeakeshouse@btinternet.com

**Mermaid Street, Rye, East Sussex TN31 7ET**

**www.jeakeshouse.com**

# Sussex

## Dacres

☎ 01323 870447

**Alfriston, East Sussex BN26 5TP**

Pretty country cottage in beautiful gardens in picturesque village. Sleeps two/three. Organic vegetarian breakfasts. En-suite bathroom. Colour TV. Tea/coffee making facilities. Near to South Downs Way, Glyndebourne, Seven Sisters, Charleston  Farmhouse, village pubs, restaurants. Wonderful walking country. PH INS CatB DA Ve CN Acc3

## Paskins Town House

☎ 01273 601203, fax 01273 621973

**18/19 Charlotte Street, Brighton, East Sussex BN2 1AG**

e-mail: welcome@paskins.co.uk
website: www.paskins.co.uk

See display ad on page 24.
H/G INS CatA Ve pNS Acc34

## Jeake's House Hotel

☎ 01797 222828, fax 01797 222623

**Mermaid Street, Rye, East Sussex TN31 7ET**

e-mail: stay@jeakeshouse.com
website: www.jeakeshouse.com

See display ad on page 24.
G INS CatA L NS Acc22

# The Silverdale
☎ 01323 491849, fax 01323 890854
## 21 Sutton Park Road, Seaford, East Sussex BN25 1RH
e-mail: silverdale@mistral.co.uk
website: www.silverdaleseaford.co.uk

Town centre house-hotel with the facilities of a hotel and the prices of a guest house. We pride ourselves on a healthy eating attitude, whilst still catering for fish and meat eaters. We are also a very pet-friendly establishment.
G INS CatB L Ve NS Acc17

## *Cafés, restaurants, pubs*

**Food for Friends** ☎ 01273 202310
  17-18 Prince Albert Street, The Lanes, Brighton, East Sussex BN1 1HF          R L c w org

**Infinity Foods Organic Café** ☎ 01273 670743
  50 Gardner Street, Brighton, East Sussex BN1 1UN
  Stunning seasonal organic food with an emphasis on fresh local produce. Nutritional awareness, outside seating, baby changing facilities, easy access. Visit our website www.infinityfoods.co.uk          C c w org

**Iydea** ☎ 01273 667992
  17 Kensington Gardens, Brighton, East Sussex BN1 4AL          C L c w

**Terre à Terre Restaurant** ☎ 01273 729051
  71 East Street, Brighton, East Sussex BN1 1HQ
  Award winning restaurant with knock-your-socks-off food, organic wine list and great service. Website www.terreaterre.co.uk          R L c org

**Café Paradiso** ☎ 01243 532967
  5 The Boardwalk, Northgate, Chichester, West Sussex PO19 1AR          R/C c

**St Martin's Organic Tearooms** ☎ 01243 786715
  3 St Martin's Street, Chichester, West Sussex PO19 1NP          C L a w org

**Wealden Wholefoods Co-op** ☎ 01892 783065
  High Street, Wadhurst, East Sussex TN5 6AA          C L b w org

# West Country

## *Cornwall*

### Coast
☎ 01736 795918

**St Ives Road, Carbis Bay, St Ives TR26 2RT**

e-mail: info@coastcornwall.co.uk
website: www.coastcornwall.co.uk

Stylish B&B, exclusively vegetarian
and vegan, all rooms en-suite, stunning
sea views and garden. Home to the
hugely popular Bean Inn Restaurant
and Wild Planet Art Gallery. Close to
St Ives beaches, restaurants and
galleries.
G CatB V Ve NS Acc16

### The Yellow House
☎ 01872 553168

**41 Vicarage Road, St Agnes TR5 0TG**

e-mail: yellowhouse41@gmail.com
website: www.stagnesyellowhouse.co.uk

Small friendly vegetarian/vegan B&B in the heart of the village.
'Excellent! Spotless rooms and a warm welcome. Veggie breakfast
cooked with love!' St Ives, Penzance and the Eden Project are less than
an hour away. Evening meals available.
G CatB V Ve NS CN Acc3

### Mount Pleasant Farm
☎ 01726 843918

**Gorran High Lanes, St Austell PL26 6LR**

e-mail: jill@mpfarm.aquiss.com
website: www.vegetarian-cornwall.co.uk

Enjoy the peace and quiet of the Cornish countryside relaxing at our
comfortable eco-friendly organic smallholding, one mile from the

beach. The Eden Project and the Lost Gardens of Heligan are nearby. We serve organic breakfasts and as vegetarian proprietors vegetarian/vegan food is our speciality. Healing and meditation also offered. ETC 3 Diamonds, Gold Green Tourism Award.
PH INS CatB Ve NS Acc6

## The Great Escape

☎ 01736 794617

### 16 Parc Avenue, St Ives TR26 2DN

website: www.g-escape.freeuk.com

Chintz-free B&B fifteen minutes from the Tate Gallery. Stunning views of St Ives Harbour and Bay. En-suite rooms with TV and CD players. Full breakfasts including freshly squeezed orange juice, full veggie/vegan fry-up and home-made yoghurt and muesli.
G INS CatB V Ve NS Acc8

## Making Waves Vegan Guest House

☎ 01736 793895

### 3 Richmond Place, St Ives TR26 1JN

e-mail: simon@making-waves.co.uk
website: www.making-waves.co.uk

Beautiful eco-renovated Victorian house. Stunning Bay and tropical garden views. Sunny patio and tiny wild garden. Relaxed, friendly atmosphere. Two minutes' stroll to harbour, five to many glorious beaches, Tate Gallery, coast path. Food is 100% animal-free, virtually all organic, and yummy!

Special diets catered for. Children and non-vegans welcome. Voted Best Vegan Guest House 1999-2000 – Vegan Magazine. Yoga courses/classes and alternative therapies available locally. Self-catering accommodation also available in our luxury sunny apartments with garden and fantastic sea views.

G INS CatB Vegan NS Acc6

# Turning Tide Vegetarian Guest House
☎ 01736 799267

## 28 Trenwith Place, St Ives TR26 1QD

e-mail: MrsShantyB@aol.com

"the place to rest and relax" A magical homely space to stay with many surprises. Stunning views from the bedroom and roof terrace. Quiet and central. Delicious healthy breakfasts with home-made soda bread. Vegetarian story suppers with storyteller Shanty Baba.

G INS CatB V Ve NS Acc2

# Michael House
☎ 01840 770592

## Trelake Lane, Treknow, Tintagel PL34 0EW

e-mail: info@michael-house.co.uk
website: www.michael-house.co.uk

Vegetarian and vegan guest house, near Tintagel, beach and coastpath nearby, lovely scenery and views, great sunsets. Evening meals, relaxing atmosphere, friendly and welcoming, open all year. Special Christmas breaks and spring and autumn offers. Children and pets welcome.

G CatB L V Ve NS CN Acc6

# Boswednack Manor
☎ 01736 794183

## Zennor, St Ives TR26 3DD

e-mail: boswednack@ravenfield.co.uk
website: www.boswednackmanor.co.uk

Peaceful farmhouse and self-catering cottage in far West Cornwall. Lovely views from all rooms. Library, organic gardens, friendly hens, sea sunsets. Wonderful walks from the door, secret coves, birds, wildflowers, stone circles. Pub ½ mile. Sorry, no dogs.

G INS CatB V Ve NS Acc10

## Cafés, restaurants, pubs

**The Bean Inn** ☎ 01736 795918
  Coast B&B, St Ives Road, Carbis Bay, St Ives TR26 2RT
  See display advert below. R/C c org

**The Golden Lion Inn and Lakeside Restaurant** ☎ 01209 860332
  Stithians Lake, Menherion, nr Redruth TR16 6NW R/P L a

**Archie Browns Café** ☎ 01736 362828
  Old Brewery Yard, Bread Street, Penzance TR18 2EQ
  Thriving café and healthfood shop providing fresh vegan and
  vegetarian food daily using local and organic produce whenever
  possible. Café open Monday to Saturday 9.30 till 5pm. Ring for
  evening opening. C L c org

**Waves Restaurant** ☎ 01841 520096
  Higher Harlyn, St Merryn, Padstow PL28 8SG R L a

**The Crooked Inn** ☎ 01752 848177
  Stoketon Cross, Trematon PL12 4RZ P L a org

**Chantek Thai & South East Asian Restaurant** ☎ 01872 225071
  15 New Bridge Street, Truro TR1 2AA
  Love authentic Asian food? Experience our open kitchen, 40+ vegetarian
  dishes, £10 pre-theatre menu, fresh juices and cooking school. R L a

**The Feast** ☎ 01872 272546
  15 Kenwyn Street, Truro TR1 3BU                    R L c w org
**Fodders Restaurant** ☎ 01872 271384
  Pannier Market, Back Quay, Truro TR1 2LL           R L a w

# Devon

## Cuddyford B & 'BEES'          ☎ 01364 653325
### Rew Road, Broadpark, Ashburton TQ13 7EN

Rural setting within Dartmoor
National Park. Ideal for exploring
Dartmoor, Dart Valley and South
Devon coastline. Wholesome
cookery – home-baked bread, free-
range eggs, honey from our own
hives, organic fruit and vegetables.
Special diets catered for. Children
are welcome.
PH INS CatB V Ve NS CN Acc4+children

## Tor Cottage          ☎ 01822 860248, fax 01822 860126
### Chillaton PL16 0JE (Tavistock/Dartmoor area)

e-mail: info@torcottage.co.uk
website: www.torcottage.co.uk

Nestling in private valley,
relaxed romantic atmosphere.
Luxurious beautiful bedsitting
en-suites with own log fires
and private gardens in stream-
side setting. Superb vegetarian
breakfasts. Vegetarian owner. RAC 5 Diamonds Little Gem Award,
National winner ETC Gold Excellence Award, 2002 All England
Winner of AA Best Accommodation Award. Heated outdoor pool.
Brochure available. Early booking advisable. See also page 10.
H INS CatA Ve NS CN Acc10

# The Royal Marine Public House & Hotel

☎ 01271 882470, fax 01271 889198

## Seaside, Combe Martin EX34 0AW

e-mail: theroyal.marine@btconnect.com
website: www.theroyalmarine.co.uk

Overlooking Combe Martin Bay, this Free House and Hotel offers comfortable and tastefully furnished en-suite bedrooms, most of which look onto the beach, Hangman Cliffs, or both. The menu is varied and we use local produce to maintain high quality and freshness.

H INS CatB L DA Ve NS Acc24

# Combe House – Hotel & Restaurant

☎ 01404 540400

**Gittisham, Honiton, nr Exeter EX14 3AD**

e-mail: stay@thishotel.com
website: www.thishotel.com

See display ad on page 32.
H INS CatA L DA Ve NS CN Acc32

# Fern Tor Vegetarian and Vegan Guest House

☎ 01769 550339

**Meshaw, South Molton EX36 4NA**

e-mail: veg@ferntor.co.uk
website: www.ferntor.co.uk

Surrounded by splendid countryside. Relax in our 12 acres or explore Exmoor, North and Mid-Devon. En-suite rooms with king size beds. Cordon Vert host. Pets welcome. Awarded 'Best Vegetarian Bed and Breakfast – 2006' by Peta.
G CatB V Ve NS Acc6

# Sparrowhawk Backpackers

☎ 01647 440318

**45 Ford Street, Moretonhampstead, Dartmoor National Park TQ13 8LN**

e-mail: ali@sparrowhawkbackpackers.co.uk
website: www.sparrowhawkbackpackers.co.uk

Small, friendly, eco-backpackers. Beautifully converted stable to wine and dine in after a hard day's hiking, biking and climbing over those magnificent Tors and Moors of Dartmoor. The kitchen is fully equipped and only for vegetarian cooking. Solar-heated showers.

Individuals, groups, families, bikes and boggy boots all welcome. A place to be yourself, read books and chat! Village centre location.
PH INS CatC DA V Ve Acc18

# Devon Valley Retreat

☎ 01548 821180

## Lower Norris House, North Huish, South Brent, nr Totnes TQ10 9NJ

e-mail: touchofheaven888@yahoo.co.uk
website: www.devon-valley-retreat.co.uk

Unwind in tranquil, green valley 8 miles from Totnes. Enjoy the lovely views from the house or relax by the log fires. Wonderful walking area. Delicious vegetarian/vegan home cooking, special diets catered for.
Healing, massage and other therapies available on request.
See also page 9.
PH INS CatB V Ve NS CN Acc6

# Berkeley's of St James

☎ and fax 01752 221654

## 4 St James Place East, The Hoe, Plymouth PL1 3AS

e-mail: enquiry@onthehoe.co.uk
website: www.onthehoe.co.uk

Quiet exclusive bed & breakfast offering free range/organic food where possible. Ideally situated on the Hoe, walking distance to Sea Front, Historic Barbican, Ferry Port, Theatre, Pavilions and City Centre and within travelling distance of the Eden Project and Dartmoor National Park.

G INS CatA DA NS CN Acc10

# Avalon – A Haven for Non-Smokers

☎ 01395 513443

## Vicarage Road, Sidmouth EX10 8UQ

e-mail: owneravalon@aol.com
website: www.avalonsidmouth.co.uk

No smoking. No children. No pets. A level walk from town centre and seafront but backing onto beautiful National Trust Park and the River Sid. One room with fourposter. Choose Avalon for service as it used to be, spotless accommodation and good wholesome food.
G INS CatB Ve NS Acc8

# The Old Forge at Totnes

☎ 01803 862174

## Seymour Place, Totnes TQ9 5AY

e-mail: enq@oldforgetotnes.com
website: www.oldforgetotnes.com

A warm and friendly 600-year-old stone building with cobbled drive and coach arch leading into a walled garden. Quiet and peaceful, yet close to town centre and river. Newly refurbished, cottage-style rooms, conservatory lounge with whirlpool spa.

Parking. Laptop users: free broadband internet access via wireless hot spot.
G INS CatA L Ve NS Acc24

## *Cafés, restaurants, pubs*

**The Terrace Café** ☎ 01626 832223
Devon Guild of Craftsmen, Riverside Mill, Bovey Tracey TQ13 9AF
C L a w org

**The Courtyard Café & Shop** ☎ 01647 432571
76 The Square, Chagford TQ13 8AE
C c w org

**Herbies Restaurant** ☎ 01392 258473
15 North Street, Exeter EX4 3QS
C L c

**The Plant Café-Deli** ☎ 01392 428144
  1 Cathedral Yard, Exeter EX1 1HJ
  Contemporary vegetarian and organic food with a wonderful view of the Cathedral. Private dinner parties and outside catering available.

C c w org

**The Country Table Café** ☎ 01626 202120
  12 Bank Street, Newton Abbot TQ12 2JW                                    C a w

**Peter Tavy Inn** ☎ 01822 810348
  Peter Tavy, nr Tavistock PL19 9NN
  See display ad above.                                                     P L a

**Plymouth Arts Centre Vegetarian Restaurant** ☎ 01752 202616
  38 Looe Street, Plymouth PL4 0EB                                      R/C L c w

**Willow Vegetarian Garden Restaurant** ☎ 01803 862605
  87 High Street, Totnes TQ9 5PB                                       R L c w org

# Dorset (West)

## Cafés, restaurants, pubs

**The Green Yard Café** ☎ 01308 459466
4-6 Barrack Street, Bridport DT6 3LY            C L a w org
**Broadwindsor Craft and Design Centre** ☎ 01308 868362
Broadwindsor, nr Beaminster DT8 3PX            R L a w
**Pilot Boat Inn** ☎ 01297 443157
Bridge Street, Lyme Regis DT7 3QA              P L a

# Somerset and Bristol

## Marlborough House ☎ 01225 318175, fax 01225 466127
### 1 Marlborough Lane, Bath BA1 2NQ

e-mail: mars@manque.dircon.co.uk
website: www.marlborough-house.net

See display ad below.
G INS CatA L DA V Ve NS Acc17

# Number 30

☎ and fax 01225 337393

## 30 Crescent Gardens, Bath BA1 2NB

e-mail: david.greenwood12@btinternet.com
website: www.numberthirty.com

Three minutes' level walk to historical city centre and private parking.
Victorian, non-smoking house with a clean, contemporary feel.
Comfortable, light en-suite bedrooms. Superb English or great
vegetarian breakfasts. 'Outstanding housekeeping with a warm
welcome.' Weekends 2 night minimum.
G INS CatA Ve NS Acc8

# Tordown

☎ 01458 832287, fax 01458 831100

## 5 Ashwell Lane, Glastonbury BA6 8BG

e-mail: torangel@aol.com
website: www.tordown.com

Victorian house situated on the
southern slopes of Glastonbury Tor.
Warm welcoming sacred space, in
which you can relax and enjoy your
stay. Beautiful rooms with tea,
coffee, herbal tea, TV, en-suite.
Healing and hydrotherapy spa
available. Sumptuous vegetarian/vegan breakfast provided. VB 4 Stars.
G INS CatB DA V Ve NS CN Acc14

# Parsonage Farm

☎ 01278 733237

## Over Stowey, Bridgwater TA5 1HA

e-mail: suki@parsonfarm.co.uk
website: www.parsonfarm.co.uk

Traditional 17th-century farmhouse
and organic smallholding in the
Quantock Hills. Friendly and
informal, with delicious meals using

farm's produce, home-made breads and jams. Peaceful village, log fires and walled gardens make your stay a relaxing break, while being ideally situated for rambling and exploring the unspoiled Quantock Hills, Exmoor, North Somerset coast, Glastonbury and Wells.
G INS CatB Ve NS CN Acc6

# The Lorna Doone Hotel

☎ 01643 862404, fax 01643 863018

### High Street, Porlock TA24 8PS

e-mail: info@lornadoonehotel.co.uk
website: www.lornadoonehotel.co.uk

Village centre hotel with 13 rooms, all en-suite with colour TV and tea/coffee facilities. We have at least 5 vegetarian choices and can offer vegan and coeliac dishes in addition to our extensive à la carte menu.
H CatB L DA Ve NS Acc30

## *Cafés, restaurants, pubs*

**Demuths Vegetarian Restaurant** ☎ 01225 446059
  2 North Parade Passage, off Abbey Green, Bath BA1 1NX
  Bath's only vegetarian restaurant. Delicious food, lots of vegan choices, organic wines. Open for breakfast, lunch and dinner. Website www.demuths.co.uk                                    R L c org
**The Porter** ☎ 01225 404445
  15 George Street, Bath BA1 2EN
  See display ad on page 40.                                    P L c
**Sally Lunn's Refreshment House** ☎ 01225 461634
  4 North Parade Passage, Bath BA1 1NX            R L a
**Tilleys Bistro** ☎ 01225 484200
  3 North Parade Passage, Bath BA1 1NX
  City centre family-run bistro. Extensive vegetarian choices – special early dinner menu for pre-theatre. See website www.tilleysbistro.co.uk
                                                              R L a
**Walrus & Carpenter** ☎ 01225 314864
  28 Barton Street, Bath BA1 1HH                    R L a
**Yum Yum Thai Restaurant** ☎ 01225 445253
  17 Kingsmead Square, Bath BA1 2AE            R L a org

**Café Kino** ☎ 0117 924 9200
  3 Ninetree Hill, Bristol BS1 3S                     C L d w org
**Café Maitreya** ☎ 0117 951 0100
  89 St Mark's Road, Easton, Bristol BS5 6HY
  The UK's top vegetarian restaurant – Which Good Food Guide, Observer Food Magazine, and the Vegetarian Society. Evenings only. Website www.cafemaitreya.co.uk                     R L c org
**Friary Café** ☎ 0117 973 3664
  9 Cotham Hill, Cotham, Bristol BS6 6LD                     C a
**One Stop Thali Café** ☎ 0117 942 6687
  12 York Road, Montpelier, Bristol BS6 5QE                     R L c
**Royce Rolls Wholefood Café** ☎ 07807 518356/0117 982 4228
  The Corn Exchange, St Nicholas Market, Bristol BS1 1JQ   C c w org
**Walrus & Carpenter** ☎ 0117 974 3793
  1 Regents Street, Clifton, Bristol BS8 4HW                     R L a
**Yum Yum Thai Restaurant** ☎ 0117 929 0987
  50 Park Street, Bristol BS1 5JN                     R L a org
**The Garden Café** ☎ 01373 454178
  16 Stony Street, Frome BA11 1BU                     R/C L c w org

**Café Galatea** ☎ 01458 834284
5A High Street, Glastonbury BA6 9DP
Established 14 years – internationally known
restaurant/gallery/cybercafé. High class vegetarian/vegan cuisine,
organic wines and beers. Open daytime and evenings. Website
www.cafegalatea.co.uk                                    R/C L c w org
**The Mitre Inn** ☎ 01458 831203
27 Benedict Street, Glastonbury BA6 9NE                    P L a
**Rainbows End Café** ☎ 01458 833896
17A High Street, Glastonbury BA6 9DP                       C c w org
**Lotus Flower Thai Restaurant** ☎ 01823 324411
89-91 Station Road, Taunton TA1 1PB                        R L a org
**The Crown at Wells & Anton's Bistrot** ☎ 01749 673457
Market Place, Wells BA5 2RP                                R/P L a

# *Wiltshire*

# Bradford Old Windmill

☎ 01225 866842, fax 01225 866648
**4 Masons Lane, Bradford on Avon, nr Bath BA15 1QN**
e-mail: vegvis@bradfordoldwindmill.co.uk
website: www.bradfordoldwindmill.co.uk

A touch of romance
near Bath in an ex-
windmill. Dramatic
position above an old
Cotswold stone town,
with spectacular views.
Vegetarian/ vegan
breakfast menu 95%
organic. Vegetarian
dinner from around the
world (Monday,
Wednesday, Thursday,
Saturday) 70% organic. Vegetarian proprietor. AA 5 Stars, Distinctly
Different 4Ds.
PH INS CatA Ve NS Acc10

## Cafés, restaurants, pubs

**Circle Restaurant** ☎ 01672 539514
  High Street, Avebury SN8 1RF                                                C L c
**The Bridge Tea Rooms** ☎ 01225 865537
  24A Bridge Street, Bradford on Avon, nr Bath BA15 1BY      R L a w
**The Bistro** ☎ 01380 720043
  7 Little Brittox, Devizes SN10 1AR                                    R L a w org
**The Cross Keys Inn** ☎ 01672 870678
  16 High Street, Great Bedwyn, Marlborough SN8 3NU
  Featured in the Guardian newspaper article 'Best Vegetarian
  Restaurants in the West Country'. Lovely, oak-beamed 16th-century
  country pub. www.thexkeys.com                                    P L a
**Anokaa** ☎ 01722 414142
  60 Fisherton Street, Salisbury SP2 7RB
  An explosive fusion of exotic spices; a rich amalgam of evocative
  aromas; a tantalising contrast of textures and tastes. Innovative
  vegetarian selections cooked by a team of professional chefs.    R L a

# Thames and Chilterns

## Bedfordshire

*Cafés, restaurants, pubs*

**Donatello's** ☎ 01525 404666
   91 Dunstable Street, Ampthill MK45 2NG     R L a
**Wok n Buffet** ☎ 01582 661485
   1 Tring Road, Dunstable LU6 2PX     R L a

## Berkshire

*Cafés, restaurants, pubs*

**The Swan Inn** ☎ 01488 668326
   Lower Green, Inkpen, nr Hungerford RG17 9DX     R/P L a w org
**Café Iguana** ☎ 0118 958 1357
   11 St Mary's Butts, Reading RG1 2LN
   Quality, healthy, home-made, organic and Fairtrade cuisine. Outside
   catering and large party bookings welcome. Chilled bar upstairs,
   reggae lounge Saturdays.     R L c w org
**Global Café** ☎ 0118 958 3555
   35-39 London Street, Reading RG1 4PS     R/C L a org
**Kathmandu Kitchen** ☎ 0118 986 4000
   55-59 Whitley Street, Reading RG2 0EG     R L a
**Misugo Japanese Restaurant** ☎ 01753 833899
   83 St Leonards Road, Windsor SL4 3BZ     R L a

## Buckinghamshire

*Cafés, restaurants, pubs*

**Carlos's Portuguese Restaurant** ☎ 01296 423021
   7-11 Temple Street, Aylesbury HP20 2RN     R L a

# *Hertfordshire*

## *Cafés, restaurants, pubs*

**The Waffle House** ☎ 01727 853502
Kingsbury Watermill, St Michaels Street, St Albans AL3 4SJ   R a org

# *Oxfordshire*

## *Cafés, restaurants, pubs*

**Café Quay** ☎ 01295 270444
Banbury Museum, Spiceball Park Road, Banbury OX16 2PQ   C L a
**Bar Meze Turkish Cuisine** ☎ 01865 761106
146 London Road, Headington, Oxford OX3 9ED   R L a
**Chiang Mai Kitchen** ☎ 01865 202233
Kemp Hall Passage, 130A High Street, Oxford OX1 4DH   R L a
**Edamame Japanese Home Cooking** ☎ 01865 246916
15 Holywell Street, Oxford OX1 3SA   R L a
**Hi-Lo Jamaican Eating House** ☎ 01865 725984
68-70 Cowley Road, Oxford OX4 1JB
Family restaurant, opened 1981. Two organic vegan dishes daily.
Veggie snacks and starters. Tropical fruits and home-made vegan ices.
R/C/P L a org
**The Magic Café** ☎ 01865 794604
110 Magdalen Road, Oxford OX4 1RQ
Friendly neighbourhood café: families welcome. Delicious lunches,
cakes and desserts, all freshly prepared on the premises. Monday-
Saturday 10am-6pm.   R/C c w org
**Modern Art Oxford** ☎ 01865 722733
30 Pembroke Street, Oxford OX1 1BP   C L b
**The Nosebag Restaurant** ☎ 01865 721033
6-8 St Michael's Street, Oxford OX1 2DU   R L a
**Vaults & Garden** ☎ 01865 279112
University Church of St Mary, High Street, Oxford OX1 4AH
C L a org

# East Anglia

## Cambridgeshire

### Stockyard Farm B&B

☎ 01354 610433, fax 01354 610422

**Wisbech Road, Welney, Wisbech PE14 9RQ**

Former farmhouse, rurally situated between Ely and Wisbech. Private lounge. 1 twin, 1 double, both with H&C, tea making, radios, hairdryers. Central heating, private parking. Pets welcome. Ideal for birdwatchers and general touring, close to Welney Wetland Centre and Ely. PH CatB Ve NS CN Acc4

### *Cafés, restaurants, pubs*

**Cambridge Blue** ☎ 01223 361382
   85/87 Gwydir Street, Cambridge CB1 2LG
   Genuine free house serving local real ales in a friendly, smoke-free environment. Wholesome food served everyday lunchtime and evening.                                                P L a

**Charlie Chan Restaurant** ☎ 01223 359336
   14 Regent Street, Cambridge CB2 1DB                         R L a

**Rainbow Vegetarian Café** ☎ 01223 321551
   9A Kings Parade, opposite Kings College gates, Cambridge CB2 1SJ
   World-famous, award-winning purely vegetarian and vegan restaurant, serving international innovative cuisine in the heart of historic Cambridge.                                          R/C L c

**The Pear Tree Public House** ☎ 01223 891680
   Hildersham CB21 6PU                                        P L a

**The Brewery Tap** ☎ 01733 358500
   80 Westgate, Peterborough PE1 2AA                          P L a

# Essex

## Cafés, restaurants, pubs

**The Lemon Tree** ☎ 01206 767337
  48 St Johns Street, Colchester CO2 7AD               R L a org
**Café Pulse** ☎ 01702 719222
  80 Leigh Road, Leigh on Sea SS9 1BZ               R/C L c org

# Norfolk

## Greenbanks Hotel & Country Restaurant                    ☎ 01362 687742
### Swaffham Road, Wendling NR19 2AB

e-mail: jenny@greenbankshotel.co.uk
website: www.greenbankshotel.co.uk

Family country hotel set in 10 acres of
lakes and meadowlands. Luxury rooms
with 5 ground floor suites with disabled
access. Dogs by arrangement. Large indoor
hydrotherapy swimming pool, jaccuzi and
sauna. Country restaurant with vegan and vegetarian menu, plus meat
cuisine, all using local produce. Silver Awards, Green Globe Tourism
Awards, Queens Awards for Environment.
H INS CatA L DA Ve NS CN Acc22

## Cafés, restaurants, pubs

**The Kings Arms** ☎ 01263 740341
  Westgate Street, Blakeney, Holt NR25 7NQ               P L a org
**Amandines** ☎ 01379 640449
  Norfolk House Courtyard, St Nicholas Street, Diss IP22 4LB     R/C L c
**The Greenhouse** ☎ 01603 631007
  42-46 Bethel Street, Norwich NR2 1NR
  Norwich's environment centre. Open Tuesday-Saturday 10am-5pm,
  hot food from noon. Soups, savouries, cakes, fairtrade, organic and
  local. www.GreenhouseTrust.co.uk               C L c w org
**Norwich Arts Centre** ☎ 01603 660352
  St Benedicts Street, Norwich NR2 4PG               C L a

**The Waffle House Restaurant** ☎ 01603 612790
  39 St Giles Street, Norwich NR2 1JN          R L a w org
**The Mulberry** ☎ 01842 820099
  11 Raymond Street, Thetford IP24 2EA          R L a

# *Suffolk*

## Western House                    ☎ 01787 280550
### High Street, Cavendish CO10 8AR

In lovely village, this old coaching house is well placed for visiting vil-
lages of Lavenham, Kersey and Long Melford, and for gardeners there
is Beth Chatto's by Colchester. Cavendish has three pubs which serve
food in the evening.
PH CatC V Ve NS Acc6

## Holly Tree House                    ☎ 01379 384068
### Bleach Green, Wingfield, near Diss IP21 5RG

e-mail: jdchallinor@beeb.net
website: www.hollytreehousebandb.co.uk
Attractive country cottage set in large gardens, dining room with oak
beams and antiques. Two lovely double bedrooms, en-suites. Visit us

for the Waveney Valley, Norfolk/Suffolk borders, cycling, visiting country pubs, coast (40 minutes). Solar hot water and wood burning stoves.

PH CatB V Ve NS CN Acc4

## *Cafés, restaurants, pubs*

**Six Bells Inn and Restaurant** ☎ 01359 250820
   The Green, Bardwell, Bury St Edmunds IP31 1AW      R/P L a
**The Linden Tree** ☎ 01284 754600
   7 Outnorthgate, Bury St Edmunds IP33 1JQ      R/P L a
**Kwan Thai Restaurant** ☎ 01473 253106
   14 St Nicholas Street, Ipswich IP1 1TJ      R L a
**Kwan Thai Restaurant** ☎ 01394 388338
   21a New Street, Woodbridge      R L a

# East Midlands

## Derbyshire

### Cafés, restaurants, pubs

**Scarthin Café** ☎ 01629 823456
Scarthin Books, The Promenade, Scarthin, Cromford DE4 3QF
C c w org

**Outside Café** ☎ 01433 651978
Main Road, Hathersage, Hope Valley S32 1BB
C L a

**Caudwell's Country Parlour** ☎ 01629 733185
Rowsley, Matlock DE4 2EB
C c w org

## Leicestershire

### Cafés, restaurants, pubs

**The Good Earth Restaurant** ☎ 0116 262 6260
19 Free Lane, Leicester LE1 1JX
R L c w org

**Jalsa Indian Vegetarian Restaurant** ☎ 0116 266 6186
87 Belgrave Road, Leicester LE4 6AS
R L b

**Staunton Stables Tea and Luncheon Rooms** ☎ 01332 864617
The Ferrer's Centre, Staunton Harold, nr Ashby-de-la-Zouch LE65 1RU
The original Tea Room here at Staunton Harold. Tourism Award winner, purveyors of fine food and beverages. Lunchtime reservations recommended.
C a

## Lincolnshire

## Waveney Cottage
☎ 01673 843236

### Willingham Road, Market Rasen LN8 3DN

website: www.waveneycottage.co.uk

Warm, comfortable, friendly non-smoking home, en-suite rooms and

choice of delicious breakfasts. Walking distance to all amenities, 20 metres from National Cycle Route, ideal base for exploring the unspoilt Wolds (AONB), east coast and historic city of Lincoln. Private car park.
PH INS CatB Ve NS Acc6

## *Cafés, restaurants, pubs*

**The Five Sailed Windmill & Tea Room** ☎ 01507 462136
East Street, Alford LN13 9EQ
One of the gems of rural Lincolnshire. Healthy eating in the stylish Tea Room. Beautiful working windmill producing stone-ground flours. Website www.fivesailed.co.uk and e-mail enquiries@fivesailed.co.uk                   C b w org

**Pimento Tearooms** ☎ 01522 544880
26/27 Steep Hill, Lincoln LN2 1LU
Home-made vegetarian and vegan meals and cakes, plus a comprehensive list of leaf teas and freshly roasted and ground coffees.
                                                                          C c

**Thailand No 1** ☎ 01522 537000
80-81 Bailgate, Lincoln LN1 3AR                          R L a
**The Copper Kettle** ☎ 01754 767298
29 Lumley Road, Skegness PE25 3LL                        R L a

# *Northamptonshire*

## *Cafés, restaurants, pubs*

**Balti King** ☎ 01604 637747/637171
76 Earl Street, Northampton NN1 3AX                      R a

# Nottinghamshire

## *Cafés, restaurants, pubs*

**Alley Café** ☎ 0115 955 1013
Cannon Court, Longrow, Nottingham NG1 6JE          R/C L c w org

**Encounters Restaurant** ☎ 0115 947 6841
59 Mansfield Road, Nottingham NG1 3FH                    R L a

**The Old Angel Pub** ☎ 0115 947 6735
7 Stoney Street, Nottingham NG1 1LG                       P L a

**Squeek Vegetarian Restaurant** ☎ 0115 955 5560
23-25 Heathcote Street, Nottingham NG1 3AG           R L c

**Minster Refectory** ☎ 01636 815691
Minster Centre, Church Street, Southwell NG25 0HD
A selection of vegetarian dishes always available. Pre-booked parties
catered for. Outside catering also available.                 R L a w

The Five Sailed Windmill,
Alford, Lincolnshire.

# Heart of England

## *Gloucestershire*

### Cheltenham Lawn and Pittville Gallery ☎ 01242 526638

**5 Pittville Lawn, Cheltenham GL52 2BE**

e-mail: anthea.millier@cheltenhamlawn.com
website: www.cheltenhamlawn.co.uk

Regency town house, close to
Pittville Park, Pump Room, town
centre, racecourse. Recently refur-
bished, original features, four-poster
bed. Conference room, art gallery.
Art/textile courses available.
Member of the Vegetarian Society's
Food and Drink Guild. Award-win-
ning breakfasts. Wireless internet.
See also page 10.

G INS CatA V Ve NS Acc10 (children on request)

### *Cafés, restaurants, pubs*

**Balti Spice** ☎ 01453 766454
   17 Gloucester Street, Stroud GL5 1QG                    R L a
**Mills Café Bar & Kitchen Shop** ☎ 01453 752222
   Witheys Yard, High Street, Stroud GL5 1AS              C L a w org

# *Herefordshire*

## Lower Bache House     ☎ 01568 750304

### Kimbolton, nr Leominster HR6 0ER

e-mail: leslie.wiles@care4free.net
website: www.smoothhound.co.uk/hotels/lowerbache.html

See display ad below.
PH INS CatA L DA Ve NS CN Acc6

### *Cafés, restaurants, pubs*

**The Pandy Inn** ☎ 01981 550273
  Dorstone, nr Hay-on-Wye HR3 6AN               P L a org
**Café @ All Saints** ☎ 01432 370415
  All Saints Church, High Street, Hereford HR4 7LD     C L a
**Nutters Coffee Shop** ☎ 01432 277447
  Capuchin Yard, Church Street, Hereford HR1 2LR
  See display ad on page 54.                   C L c

**Nature's Choice** ☎ 01989 763454
  Raglan House, 17 Broad Street, Ross-on-Wye HR9 7EA
  We provide a wide selection of vegetarian, vegan and gluten-free
  dishes, also bed and breakfast. www.natures-choice.biz     C L a org

# *Shropshire*

# White House Vegetarian Bed and Breakfast
                                                        ☎ 01691 658524
## Maesbury Marsh, Oswestry SY10 8JA

e-mail: whitehouse@maesburymarsh.co.uk
website: www.maesburymarsh.co.uk

See display ad on page 55.
G INS CatB DA V Ve NS Acc6+2 children

## *Cafés, restaurants, pubs*

**Cinnamon Coffee & Meeting House** ☎ 01746 762944
  Waterloo House, Cartway, Bridgnorth WV16 4EG     C L c w org

**Acorn Wholefood Café** ☎ 01694 722495
26 Sandford Avenue, Church Stretton SY6 6BW
Into its third decade – but still at the top in wholefood produce.
Recently refurbished. Winner of Platinum Healthy Eating Award.

C a w org

**Berry's Coffee House** ☎ 01694 724452
17 High Street, Church Stretton SY6 6BU                       C L a

**Cinnamon at the Green Wood Centre** ☎ 01952 432769
Station Road, Coalbrookdale, Telford TF8 7DR          C L c w org

**The Sun Inn** ☎ 01584 861239
Corfton, Craven Arms SY7 9DF
This pub offers six vegetarian dishes and one vegan dish. Real ale on
sale, one is always suitable for vegans and vegetarians.          P L a

**The Olive Branch** ☎ 01584 874314
2/4 Old Street, Ludlow SY8 1NP                        R/C L a w

**Raphaels Restaurant** ☎ 01952 461136
4 Church Street, Shifnal TF11 9AA                          R L a

**The Goodlife Wholefood Restaurant** ☎ 01743 350455
73 Barrack's Passage, Wyle Cop, Shrewsbury SY1 1XA   R/C L c w org

# Warwickshire

## Cafés, restaurants, pubs

**The Vintner** ☎ 01789 297259
  4-5 Sheep Street, Stratford-upon-Avon CV37 6EF      R/Wine bar L a
**Saffron Restaurant** ☎ 01926 402061
  Unit 1, Westgate House, Market Street, Warwick CV34 4DE      R L a

# West Midlands

## Cafés, restaurants, pubs

**Jyoti Vegetarian Restaurant** ☎ 0121 766 7199
  569-571 Stratford Road, Sparkhill, Birmingham B11 4LS      R c
**Khazana Pure Indian and Chinese Restaurant** ☎ 0121 551 0908
  12 Holyhead Road, Handsworth, Birmingham B21 0LT      R L c
**Sibila's Restaurant** ☎ 0121 456 7634
  Canal Square, 100 Browning Street, Birmingham B16 8EH   R L c w org

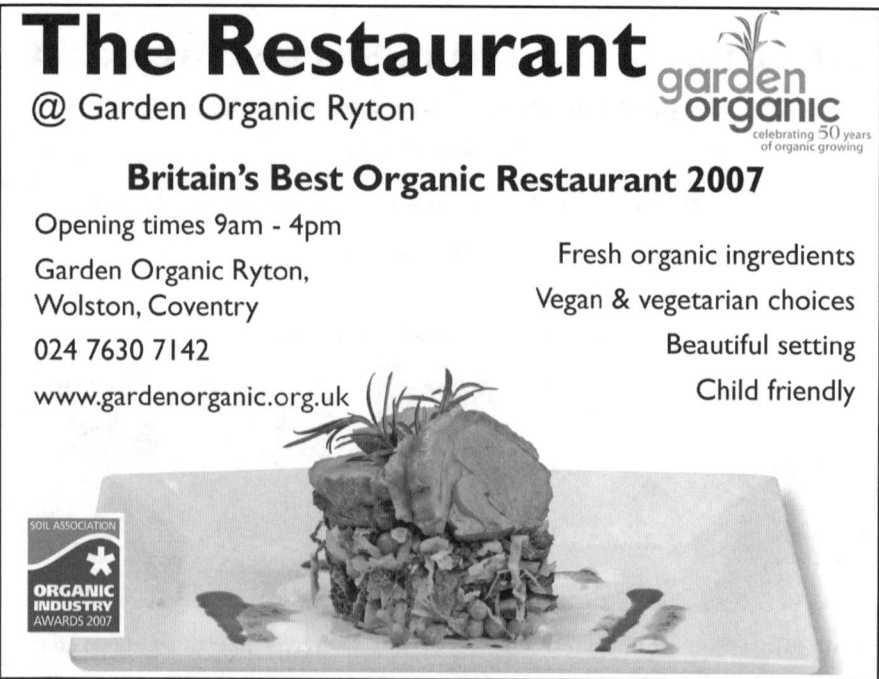

**The Warehouse Café** ☎ 0121 633 0261
54-57 Allison Street, Digbeth, Birmingham B5 5TH
City centre oasis for vegetarians and vegans. Inexpensive good quality
food, plenty of choice in laid-back surroundings.      R/C c w org
**Browns Independent Bar** ☎ 024 7622 1100
Earl Street, Coventry CV1 5RU
A family owned and run bar. One minute's walk from Coventry
Cathedral. www.brownsindependentbar.com      C L a
**Kakooti Italian Restaurant** ☎ 024 7622 1392
16 Spon Street, Coventry CV1 3BA      R L a
**The Restaurant at Garden Organic Ryton** ☎ 024 7630 7142
Wolston Lane, Ryton on Dunsmore, Coventry CV8 3LG
See display ad on page 56.      R L a org

# *Worcestershire*

## Mrs Margaret Peters, Tytchney Gables
☎ 01905 620185
### Boreley, Ombersley, nr Worcester WR9 0HZ

Sixteenth-century medieval Hall House cottage in peaceful country
lane, 2½ miles Ombersley, 8 miles Worcester. Ideal for walking and
touring. River Severn nearby and just half a
mile to Ombersley Golf Course. Double,
family and single rooms, cot

Tytchney Gables      Derek Griffin

available. B&B from £20. Only 1½ miles from the Bishops Wood
Environmental Education Centre – see page 10.
PH CatB Ve NS CN Acc6

## *Cafés, restaurants, pubs*

**Lady Foley's Tea Room** ☎ 01684 893033
  Great Malvern Station, Imperial Road, Malvern WR14 3AT     C L b
**Red Lion** ☎ 01684 564787
  4 St Anns Road, Great Malvern WR14 4RG                 P L a org
**Chesters Restaurant** ☎ 01905 611638
  51 New Street, Worcester WR1 2DL                       R L a

# North East England

## Cleveland

*Cafés, restaurants, pubs*

**Eliano's Brasserie** ☎ 01642 868566
20-22 Fairbridge Street, off Grange Road, Middlesbrough TS1 5DJ
R L a

**The Waiting Room** ☎ 01642 780465
9 Station Road, Eaglescliffe, Stockton-on-Tees TS16 0BU
The Waiting Room is a truly excellent, Observer award-winning restaurant (2007), established for 22 years. Website: www.the-waiting-room.co.uk
R L c w org

## Durham

# Polemonium Plantery
☎ 01429 881529

### 28 Sunnyside, Trimdon Grange, Trimdon Station TS29 6HF

e-mail: bandb@polemonium.co.uk
website: www.polemonium.co.uk

An environmentally-friendly (Green Tourism Gold Award) country village retreat. Family-friendly, Fairtrade, organic, with vegan toiletries. 2 miles off Cycle Route 1, 7 miles east of Durham. En-suite rooms, under 2s free with organic nappy service. See also page 10.
G INS CatB Ve NS Acc4

# Northumberland

## Cafés, restaurants, pubs

**The Hexham Tans Restaurant** ☎ 01434 656284
  13 St Marys Chare, Hexham NE46 1NQ                R L c
**The Chantry Tea Rooms** ☎ 01670 514414
  9A Chantry Place, Morpeth NE61 1PJ                C L a

# Tyne & Wear

## Cafés, restaurants, pubs

**Sky Apple Café** ☎ 0191 209 2571
  182 Heaton Road, Heaton, Newcastle upon Tyne NE6 5HP    R/C c

# Yorkshire

## Golden Lion Hotel ☎ 01969 622161, fax 01969 623836
## Market Square, Leyburn, North Yorkshire DL8 5AS

e-mail: info@goldenlionleyburn.co.uk
website: www.thegoldenlion.co.uk

Family-run traditional market square hotel set in the heart of the Yorkshire Dales. Comfortable en-suite rooms, complemented by good freshly-prepared food. Full disabled facilities – lift to all floors. A great base to discover the Dales.
H INS CatA L DA Ve pNS Acc24

# Beck Hall

☎ 01729 830332

## Cove Road, Malham, North Yorkshire BD23 4DJ

e-mail: alice@beckhallmalham.com
website: www.beckhallmalham.com

Eighteenth-century pet and child friendly Beck Hall welcomes visitors to the Yorkshire Dales. Situated by a stream and surrounded by countryside, there are 2 pubs nearby for dinner. Vegetarian home-cooked breakfasts and packed lunches.
G INS CatB L Ve NS Acc35

# Northcliff B&B

☎ 01947 880481

## Mount Pleasant North, Robin Hood's Bay, nr Whitby, North Yorkshire YO22 4RE

e-mail: northcliff@rhbay.co.uk
website: www.north-cliff.co.uk

Northcliff B&B is a lovely Victorian house in Robin Hood's Bay, on the edge of the North York Moors. We offer:
• double and twin rooms, all en-suite
• colour TVs • hospitality trays
• parking • some sea views
• secure cycle storage
• vegetarian/special diets by request.
PH CatB Ve NS Acc6

# Fountains Court Holistic Health Hotel
☎ 01723 381118, fax 01723 381181

**120 Columbus Ravine, Scarborough, North Yorkshire YO12 7QZ**

e-mail: info@fountainscourt.com
website: www.fountainscourt.com

• A quiet hotel for health breaks, retreats, complementary medicine, pampering.
• No children, Feng Shui décor, hot-tub, sauna, mini-gym and a Zen Garden.
• Delicious vegetarian/vegan menu, licensed. (Tinsel-free Christmas's!)
• A beautiful coastline location with an historic harbour-town.

*'No ordinary hotel'*

H CatA L Ve NS CN Acc16

# Marine View Guest House
☎ 01723 361864

**34 Blenheim Terrace, Scarborough, North Yorkshire YO12 7HD**

e-mail: info@marineview.co.uk
website: www.marineview.co.uk

Ian and Virginia welcome you to their friendly, family-run six bed-roomed non-licensed guest house. Set in a prominent position on the north cliff overlooking the magnificent North Bay. All of Scarborough's numerous attractions are within easy walking distance.
G INS CatB Ve NS CN Acc15

# Falcon Guesthouse
☎ 01947 603507

**29 Falcon Terrace, Whitby, North Yorkshire YO21 1EH**

B&B in quiet location, seven minutes' walk from centre and harbour. Lounge and sunny breakfast room. Organic fare. Tea making equipment in bedrooms. Parking near house. Whitby has

beach, historical connections, and proximity to North York moors.
PH CatB Ve NS Acc7

## Avondale Guest House ☎ 01904 633989
### 61 Bishopthorpe Road, York YO23 1NX

e-mail: kaleda@avondaleguesthouse.co.uk
website: www.avondaleguesthouse.co.uk

Charming 19th-century Victorian House just a few minutes' walk to York's ancient city walls. Homely en-suite rooms with extensive breakfast menu including vegetarian options. Non-smoking environment with free on-road parking. Prices from £31 pp/pn. Minimum booking two nights.
G INS CatB Ve NS Acc12

## Cornmill Lodge Vegetarian Guest House ☎ and fax 01904 620566
### 120 Haxby Road, York YO31 8JP

e-mail: cornmillyork@aol.com
website: www.cornmillyork.co.uk

A spacious Edwardian guest house within 15 minutes' walk of York Minster. Wide choice of breakfasts using organic and Fairtrade food where possible. Completely non-smoking. All bedrooms en-suite. Car parking at rear. Vegetarian owner. Discounts for vegetarian/vegan members of various environmental organisations, such as Viva!, Peta, FOE and Greenpeace.
G CatB V Ve NS Acc7

### *Cafés, restaurants, pubs*

**South Square Vegetarian Café** ☎ 01274 834928
    South Square, Thornton Road, Thornton, Bradford, West Yorkshire
    BD13 3LD                                                    C c
**Malt Shovel Inn** ☎ 01423 862929
    Brearton, Harrogate, North Yorkshire HG3 3BX                P L a
**Brook's Restaurant** ☎ 01484 715284
    6 Bradford Road, Brighouse, West Yorkshire HD6 1RW          R L a

**Eating Whole** ☎ 01302 738730
25 Copley Road, Doncaster, South Yorkshire DN1 2PE
Small, friendly. All food prepared on the premises. Varied menu.
Open Monday-Saturday 9am-4pm, also Thursday, Friday and
Saturday from 7.30pm onwards.                     R/C L c org

**Thai Elephant Restaurant** ☎ 01423 530099
Unit 3, 15 Cheltenham Parade, Harrogate, North Yorkshire HG1 1DD
                                                   R L a

**Wild Ginger** ☎ 01423 566122
5 Station Parade, Harrogate, North Yorkshire HG1 1UF
Award-winning home-cooked food that is ethical, traditional and
unique. Adventurous salads, sensational burgers, organic drinks,
home-made bread and cakes.                         C L c w org

**Laughing Gravy** ☎ 01422 844425
The Birchcliffe Centre, Birchcliffe Road, Hebden Bridge, West
Yorkshire HX7 8DG
Licensed vegetarian restaurant, open evenings Thursdays, Fridays,
Saturdays and Sundays. Bookings only, on 01422 844425.
www.laughinggravy.co.uk                            R L c

**Organic House** ☎ 01422 843429
2 Market Street, Hebden Bridge, West Yorkshire HX7 6AA
Specialist organic café and shop. Home-made food, cakes, coffees and
juices. Excellent Sunday brunch. Fresh produce, convenience foods
and household goods.                               C L c w org

**Vinehouse Café** ☎ 01439 771427
Helmsley Walled Garden, Cleveland Way, Helmsley, North Yorkshire
YO62 5AH
Delicious, unusual salads, home-made soups, home-made cakes,
Fairtrade tea and coffee, served in the peaceful surroundings of
Helmsley Walled Garden. Open daily from 1st April to 31st October
10.30am-5pm.                                       C c w org

**Hitchcock's Vegetarian Restaurant** ☎ 01482 320233
1-2 Bishop Lane, Hull, East Yorkshire HU1 1PA     R L c

**Zoo Café** ☎ 01482 494352
80B Newland Avenue, Hull, East Yorkshire HU5 3AB   C c

**Pollyanna's Tearoom** ☎ 01423 869208
Jockey Lane, Knaresborough, North Yorkshire HG5 0HF   C L a

**Hansa's Gujarati Vegetarian Restaurant** ☎ 0113 244 4408
72/74 North Street, Leeds, West Yorkshire LS2 7PN
Award-winning Indian vegetarian restaurant serving mouth-watering
Gujarati vegetarian home cooking for the past 21 years.   R L c w org
**Little Tokyo** ☎ 0113 243 9090
24 Central Road, Leeds, West Yorkshire LS1 6DE
We use separate fryer for vege food. Also serve a full range of vegetarian
and organic white and red wine, rosé and champagne.   R L a org
**The Millrace Bar & Restaurant** ☎ 0113 275 7555
2-6 Commercial Road, Leeds, West Yorkshire LS5 3AQ
Award-winning restaurant serving the best in organic and local
produce. Situated by historic Kirkstall Abbey and Leeds city centre.
   R L a org
**Roots & Fruits** ☎ 0113 242 8313
10/11 Grand Arcade, Leeds, West Yorkshire LS1 6PG
Friendly vegetarian café serving all-day breakfast. Starters,
sandwiches, jacket potatoes, mains, specials board, desserts. Many
dishes can be made vegan.   C c
**Airy Fairy** ☎ 0114 249 2090
239 London Road, Sheffield, South Yorkshire S2 4NF   C c w org
**Blue Moon Café** ☎ 0114 276 3443
2 St James Street, Sheffield, South Yorkshire S1 2EW   C L c
**The Fat Cat** ☎ 0114 249 4801
23 Alma Street, Sheffield, South Yorkshire S3 8SA
Award-winning city pub, 150-year-old listed building. Beer garden.
Vegetarian and vegan dishes a speciality. Menu changes weekly.   P L a
**Green Edge Café** ☎ 0114 258 8550
4 Nether Edge Road, Sheffield, South Yorkshire S7 1RU
Friendly local café, serving interesting, varied cuisine. Excellent home-
made cakes. Open Tues-Sat 9.30-4.30, occasional evenings. Closed
August/Christmas.   C c
**Kumquat Mae** ☎ 0114 250 1076
353 Abbeydale Road, Sheffield, South Yorkshire S7 1FS   R c
**Nirmal Restaurant** ☎ 0114 272 4054
189-193 Glossop Road, Sheffield, South Yorkshire S10 2GW   R L a
**Le Caveau Restaurant** ☎ 01756 794274
86 High Street, Skipton, North Yorkshire BD23 1JJ   R L a

**Wild Oats Café** ☎ 01756 790619

10 High Street, Skipton, North Yorkshire BD23 1JZ          C c w org

**Dandelion and Burdock** ☎ 01422 316000

16 Town Hall Street, Sowerby Bridge, West Yorkshire HX6 2EA

R L d org

**The Magpie Café** ☎ 01947 602058

14 Pier Road, Whitby, North Yorkshire YO21 3PU          R L a

**The Blake Head Bookshop & Vegetarian Café** ☎ 01904 623767

104 Micklegate, York YO1 6JX

Open 7 days a week serving breakfast, lunch and snacks. Child-friendly and disabled access. All food home-made.          C L c w org

**El Piano** ☎ 01904 610676

15-17 Grape Lane, The Quarter, York YO1 7HU

After 10 years – officially famous for gluten-free and vegan options! Over 80% of the menu is both. Varied! Delicious!          R/C L c org

**The Spurriergate Centre** ☎ 01904 629393

St Michaels Church, Spurriergate, York YO1 9QR          C a

# North West England

## Cheshire

*Cafés, restaurants, pubs*

**Sokrates Greek Taverna** ☎ 0161 282 0050
25A Northenden Road, Sale M33 2DH                    R L a

## Cumbria

# Rothay Manor          ☎ 015394 33605, fax 015394 33607
**Rothay Bridge, Ambleside LA22 0EH**

e-mail: hotel@rothaymanor.co.uk
website: www.rothaymanor.co.uk

Award-winning Country House Hotel in
the heart of the Lake District. Ideal for
walking, sightseeing or relaxing. Renowned
for the warm, friendly atmosphere; excellent
restaurant. Rooms and suites for families and disabled guests. Free use of nearby Leisure Centre. See also page 9.
H INS CatA L DA Ve NS Acc37

# Lancrigg Vegetarian Country House Hotel          ☎ 015394 35317

**Easedale, Grasmere LA22
9QN**

e-mail: info@lancrigg.co.uk
website: www.lancrigg.co.uk

Peace and relaxation in historic
country house with comfortable
accommodation. Some rooms
with whirlpool baths.
International vegetarian cuisine.

Special diets. Restaurant fully certified organic. Therapies and entry to country health spa available. Stunning mountain setting with 30 acres private grounds.
H INS CatA L V Ve NS Acc26

## Ardrig
☎ 01539 736879
### 144 Windermere Road, Kendal LA9 5EZ
website: www.ardrigvegetarian.com

Ardrig is a quiet, friendly home with clean comfortable rooms. Positively non-smoking. Breakfast is vegetarian/vegan, fresh, filling, mostly Fairtrade, organic food. Convenient for Kendal shops, restaurants, Arts Centre, museums and transport links. Bicycle store available.
PH INS CatB V Ve NS Acc5

## Park House Farm
☎ 015396 24742
### Langdale, Gaisgill, Orton, Penrith CA10 3UH
e-mail: stay@parkhousefarm.com
website: www.parkhousefarm.com

Eighteenth-century farmhouse offering: holiday cottage, Dinner B&B, camping barn and camping at an 8-acre organic farm at foot of Howgill Fells – an imposing range of unique velvet-domed hills. On the edge of the Yorkshire Dales and a stone's throw from the Lake District. See our geese and rare breed Hebridean sheep!

PH CatA V Ve NS CN Acc6-8+camping

# The Screes Hotel

☎ and fax 019467 26262

## Nether Wasdale, Seascale CA20 1ET

e-mail: info@thescreesinnwasdale.com
website: www.thescreesinnwasdale.com

The Screes Inn is situated in the heart of Wasdale in the Lake District. We are a small family-run inn accommodating up to 12 people. Johnny, our vegetarian head chef, cooks a wide range of vegetarian and some vegan food.

H INS CatA L DA Ve NS CN Acc12

# Hazel Bank Country House

☎ 017687 77248, fax 017687 77373

## Rosthwaite, Borrowdale, Keswick CA12 5XB

e-mail: enquiries@hazelbankhotel.co.uk
website: www.hazelbankhotel.co.uk

Hazel Bank stands peacefully amidst 4-acre gardens with breathtaking views of Central Lakeland. Bedrooms are luxuriously furnished, well-proportioned, fully en-suite with stunning views. AA Red Rosette for Fine Food, AA 5 Gold Stars (93% Merit Award score),

VisitBritain 5 Stars + Gold Award, RAC Little Gem 2002-2006, RAC Two Dining Awards 2002-2006. Non-smoking. No pets. See also page 9.

G INS CatA L DA Ve NS Acc16

# Nab Cottage
☎ 015394 35311, fax 015394 35493
## Rydal, Ambleside LA22 9SD

e-mail: tim@nabcottage.com
website: www.rydalwater.com

In the heart of the Lake
District, Nab Cottage is
beautifully situated overlooking
Rydal Water and surrounded
by mountains. It dates from the
16th century and has many
literary associations. Cosy,
informal atmosphere – delicious home-cooked food. Shiatsu, massage
and Reiki available. See also page 9.
G INS CatB Ve NS Acc18

# Sefton House
☎ 01229 582190
## 34 Queen Street, Ulverston LA12 7AF

e-mail: info@seftonhouse.co.uk
website: www.seftonhouse.co.uk

Sefton House is a clean and comfortable
family-run guest house, centrally located in
the traditional market town of Ulverston.
Our vegetarian breakfasts are freshly
prepared using locally-grown, organic and
Fairtrade ingredients wherever possible. We
cater for special diets.
G INS CatB V Ve NS Acc10

# St John's Lodge
☎ 015394 43078, fax 015394 88054
## Lake Road, Windermere LA23 2EQ

e-mail: mail@st-johns-lodge.co.uk
website: www.st-johns-lodge.co.uk

See display ad on page 71.
G INS CatB Ve NS Acc26

## *Cafés, restaurants, pubs*

**Siskins Café** ☎ 017687 78410
   Whinlatter Visitor Centre, Braithwaite, Keswick CA12 5TW   C L a w org
**Watermill Café** ☎ 016974 78267
   Priests Mill, Caldbeck, Wigton CA7 8DR                                    C a
**Quince & Medlar Restaurant** ☎ 01900 823579
   13 Castlegate, Cockermouth CA13 9EU                          R L c org
**The Green Valley Organic Restaurant at Lancrigg** ☎ 015394 35317
   Lancrigg, Grasmere LA22 9QN
   Fully organic. Healthy, delicious and nutritious. Special diets. Open
   every day. Breakfasts, lunches, afternoon teas, evening meals.
   Stunning location, ½ mile from Grasmere village. Website
   www.greenvalleyorganic.co.uk and e-mail
   purefood@greenvalleyorganic.co.uk                          R/C c w org
**The Quaker Tapestry and Tearooms** ☎ 01539 722975
   Quaker Tapestry Exhibition Centre, Friends Meeting House,
   Stramongate, Kendal LA9 4BH.
   See display ad on page 72.                                            C c
**The Union Jack Café** ☎ 01539 722458
   15 Kirkland, Kendal LA9 5AF                                         C L a

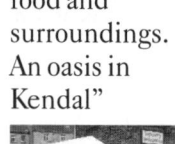

**Waterside Wholefoods Café/Restaurant & Shop** ☎ 01539 733252/729743
Kent View, Waterside, Kendal LA9 4DZ
See display ad on page 72.                                    C L c w org

**The Lakeland Pedlar Wholefood Café** ☎ 017687 74492
Hendersons Yard, Bell Close, Keswick CA12 5JD
See display ad above.                                        R/C L c w org

**Maysons Restaurant** ☎ 017687 74104
33 Lake Road, Keswick CA12 5DQ                               R/C L a

**The Watermill** ☎ 01768 881523
Little Salkeld, Penrith CA10 1NN
See display ad on page 74.                                    C c w org

**The Village Bakery** ☎ 01768 881811
Melmerby, nr Penrith CA10 1HE
Organic restaurant and bakeshop specialising in products suitable for people with special diet requirements. Open all year (excluding Christmas and New Year).                     R/C L a w org

**Mardale Inn** ☎ 01931 713244
Bampton, Penrith CA10 2RQ                                     P L a

# *Isle of Man*

## Fernleigh
☎ and fax 01624 842435

### Marine Parade, Peel IM5 1PB

e-mail: fernleigh@manx.net
website: www.isleofman.com/accommodation/fernleigh

Looking across the bay, in the quiet fishing village of Peel. Join us in our comfortable

PEEL CASTLE

Victorian home on the sea front, standard and en-suite rooms. Complemented by our excellent choice of home-made vegetarian and traditional breakfasts. Standard room £23.00, en-suite £28.00 p.p.p.n. G INS CatB Ve NS Acc22

## *Cafés, restaurants, pubs*

**Greens Vegetarian Restaurant** ☎ 01624 629129
Steam Railway Station, Bank Hill, Douglas IM1 4LL     R/C L c

# Lancashire, Greater Manchester and Merseyside

## Cameo Hotel
☎ 01253 626144, fax 01253 296048
### 30 Hornby Road, Blackpool FY1 4QG

e-mail: enquiries@cameo-hotel.co.uk
website: www.cameo-hotel.co.uk

See display ad below.
H CatB L Ve NS Acc21

## *Cafés, restaurants, pubs*

**Red Triangle Café** ☎ 01282 832319
160 St James Street, Burnley BB11 1NR
Just off Burnley town centre, we are an informal daytime café
(Tuesday to Saturday) and a relaxed candlelit bistro for evening meals
– Fridays, Saturdays and other evenings on request. We also provide
buffets for events within travelling distance. R/C L c

**Jim's Café/The Vegetarian Restaurant** ☎ 01282 868828
  19-21 New Market Street, Colne BB8 9BJ           R L c
**Sokrates Greek Taverna** ☎ 01204 692100
  80-84 Winter Hey Lane, Horwich, Bolton BL6 7NZ      R L a
**Blackburne House Café Bar** ☎ 0151 708 3929
  Blackburne House, Blackburne Place, off Hope Street, Liverpool L8 7PE
  The relaxed ambience, eclectic mix of vegetarian and non-vegetarian dishes and wickedly tempting selection of desserts, make the Blackburne House Café Bar an experience not to be missed.    C L a
**Everyman @ Blackwell's** ☎ 0151 709 0025
  Blackwell University Bookshop, University of Liverpool, Alsop Building, Brownlow Hill, Liverpool L3 5TX
  See display ad above.                             C a
**Everyman Bistro and Bars** ☎ 0151 708 9545
  5-9 Hope Street, Liverpool L1 9BH
  See display ad on page 77.                    R/C/P L a

**Greenfish Café** ☎ 0151 707 8592
11 Upper Newington, Liverpool L1 2SR                    C c
**Yuet Ben Restaurant** ☎ 0151 709 5772
1 Upper Duke Street, Liverpool L1 9DU
Liverpool's first and original Peking-style restaurant. Same family-run
restaurant since 1968. www.yuetben.co.uk                    R L a
**Earth Vegetarian Café and Juice Bar** ☎ 0161 834 1996
16-20 Turner Street, Northern Quarter, Manchester M4 1DZ
10.00-7.00 Tuesday-Friday, 10.00-5.00 Saturday. Fresh, seasonal home
cooking. Fairtrade, vegan, ethical food, juices and drinks.                    C d
**Everyman @ Blackwell's** ☎ 0161 273 8000
Blackwell University Bookshop, The Precinct Centre, Oxford Road,
Manchester M13 9RN
See display ad on page 76.                    C a
**On the Eighth Day Vegetarian Health Food Shop and Café**
☎ 0161 273 4878
111 Oxford Road, Manchester M1 7DU                    C L c

**Tampopo** ☎ 0161 819 1966
16 Albert Square, Manchester M2 5PF                    R L a
**Bear Café** ☎ 01706 813737
29 Rochdale Road, Todmorden OL14 7LA
Beautiful first-floor café/restaurant in period building. All food
cooked on premises or locally. Parties catered for. Outside catering.
R/C c w org

# Wales

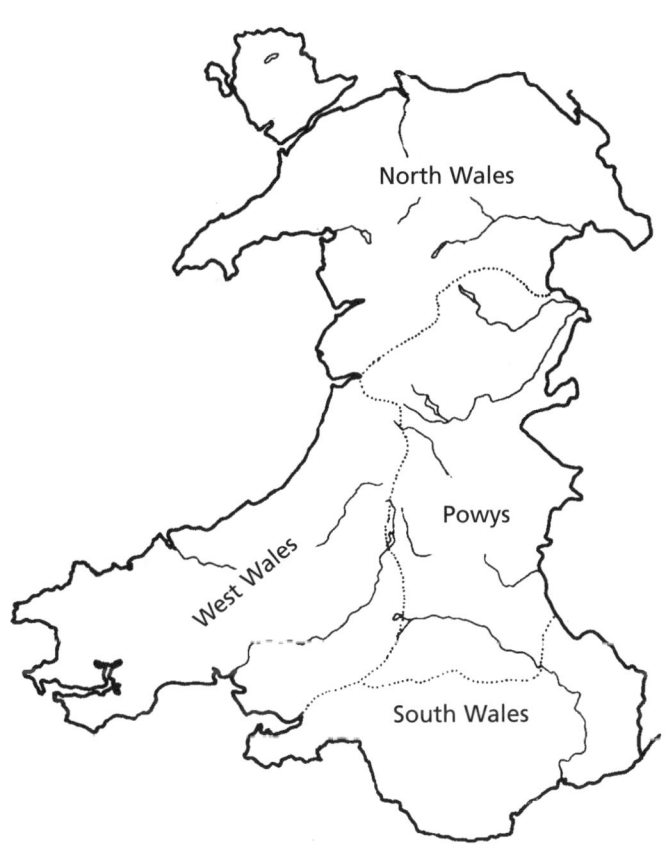

North Wales

West Wales

Powys

South Wales

## Ivy House

☎ 01341 422535, fax 01341 422689

### Finsbury Square, Dolgellau, Gwynedd LL40 1RF

e-mail: marg.bamford@btconnect.com
website: www.ivyhouse-dolgellau.co.uk

Country town guest house offering attractive accommodation, good food and a welcoming atmosphere. The six bedrooms have TV, hairdryers and tea/coffee facilities, four of them have en-suite facilities. Delicious

vegetarian/traditional breakfasts and evening meals. Open all year.
G INS CatB Ve NS Acc13

# Tremeifion Vegetarian Hotel

☎ 01766 770491

**Soar Road, Talsarnau, nr Harlech, Gwynedd LL47 6UH**

e-mail: enquire@vegetarian-hotel.com
website: www.vegetarian-hotel.com

See display ad on page 80.
H CatA L V Ve NS CN Acc10

## *Cafés, restaurants, pubs*

**Alpine Coffee Shop and Gallery** ☎ 01690 710747
   Station Approach, Betws-y-Coed, Gwynedd LL24 0AE     C a w org

# *Powys*

# Trericket Mill Vegetarian Guest House, Bunkhouse & Camping

☎ 01982 560312

**Erwood, Builth Wells LD2 3TQ**

e-mail: mail@trericket.co.uk
website: www.trericket.co.uk

We offer a range of accommodation overlooking the River Wye, from camping and bunkroom, with optional bedding and breakfast, to en-suite bed and wholesome vegetarian breakfast in our grade 2* listed corn mill and cosy bunkhouse set in an old  cider orchard beside the mill stream. Small but friendly! Contact Nicky or Alistair Legge. See also page 12.
G INS CatB V Ve NS Acc16+camping

# Elan Valley Hotel ☎ 01597 810448, fax 01597 810824
## Elan Valley, nr Rhayader LD6 5HN

e-mail: info@elanvalleyhotel.co.uk
website: www.elanvalleyhotel.co.uk

See display ad on page 83 and also page 12.
H INS CatA L DA Ve NS Acc20+

# The Old Post Office ☎ 01497 820008
## Llanigon, Hay-on-Wye HR3 5QA

website: www.oldpost-office.co.uk

See display ad on page 83.
G CatB V Ve NS CN Acc6

# Gwalia Farm ☎ 01650 511377
## Cemmaes, Machynlleth SY20 9PZ

website: www.gwaliafarm.co.uk

Peaceful, remote small farm with goats, hens, sheep. Beautiful views of mountains of southern Snowdonia. Centre for Alternative Technology nearby. Home-cooked wholefood meals using our own organic vegetables, fruit, milk, eggs. B&B £25, also self-catering caravan and camping. Spring water, log fire, lake, excellent walking, birdwatching, and silence!
PH CatB V Ve NS CN Acc5+s/c caravan and camping

## *Cafés, restaurants, pubs*

**The Quarry Café** ☎ 01654 702624
   13 Heol Maengwyn, Machynlleth SY20 8EB     C c w org
**The Hat Shop Restaurant** ☎ 01544 260017
   7 High Street, Presteigne LD8 2BA     R L a w org
**Carole's Tearoom & Cake Shop** ☎ 01597 811060
   Old Swan, West Street, Rhayader LD6 5AB     C a

## Awen Vegetarian B&B

☎ 01495 244615/07905 148108

### Penrhiwgwair Cottage, Twyn Road, Abercarn, Newport, Gwent NP11 5AS

e-mail: info@awenbandb.com
website: www.awenbandb.com

Historic 16th-century Welsh longhouse with log fires and oak beams. Breathtaking scenery and mountain walks. Two family rooms, one with romantic four-poster bed. Vegan and special diets welcome. Evening meals and lunchboxes available.

Organic, Fairtrade and ecofriendly owners. See also page 11.
G INS CatB V Ve NS Acc5

*Cafés, restaurants, pubs*

**Hunky Dory** ☎ 01633 257850
   17 Charles Street, Newport, Gwent NP20 5EE        R c w org

**Chapter Café** ☎ 029 2031 1050
   Chapter Arts Centre, Market Road, Canton, Cardiff, South
   Glamorgan CF5 1QE        C L a org

**Crumbs** ☎ 02920 395007
   33 Morgan Arcade, Cardiff, South Glamorgan CF10 1AF
   DO YOUR BODY A FAVOUR – EAT 'CRUMBS'! Established 1970
   by present proprietor Judi. Home-made salads and hot food. All
   veggie – some vegan, wheat- and dairy-free.        R c

**Embassy Café** ☎ 02920 373144
   @ Cathays Community Centre, 36 Cathays Terrace, Cardiff, South
   Glamorgan CF24 4HX        C c org

**Govinda's Vegetarian Restaurant** ☎ 01792 468469
   8 Cradock Street, Swansea, West Glamorgan SA1 3EN        R c org

## Heartspring      ☎ 01267 241999

**Hill House, Llansteffan, nr Carmarthen,
Carmarthenshire SA33 5JG**

e-mail: info@heartspring.co.uk
website: www.heartspring.co.uk

Magical Retreat Centre superbly situated overlooking a stunning coastal conservation area. Exclusively vegan/vegetarian and 100% organic with our own spring water, and no smoking throughout. We offer retreats (not aligned to any religion) and self-contained apartments for peaceful and healing holidays with the option of nurturing sessions with our team of professional complementary practitioners. See also page 11.
Retreat Centre CatA V Ve NS Acc14

## Rhyd-y-Groes B&B      ☎ and fax 01570 470188

**Bwlchllan, Lampeter, Ceredigion SA48 8QN**

e-mail: enquiries@rhyd-y-groes.com
website: www.rhyd-y-groes.com

Peaceful 4 Star accommodation in rural setting with panoramic views of surrounding countryside, easily accessible from the B4337. Hot Tub/Spa, aromatherapy available. Convenient base for relaxing or activity breaks. Local wildlife includes red kites, dolphins and seals. Enjoy an evening meal in the newly renovated restaurant, seasonal alfresco dining and BBQs in restaurant garden. Vegetarian menu, speciality home-baked bread, fresh duck eggs when laying. Vegetarian Society accredited, bronze Welsh Food Hygiene Award. Equine B&B also available.
PH INS CatB Ve NS CN Acc8

# Glanhelyg

☎ 01239 682119/682482

## Llechryd, Cardigan, Ceredigion SA43 2NJ

e-mail: ksapey@tiscali.co.uk
website: www.glanhelyg.co.uk

Quiet location within easy reach of Cardigan, beaches and countryside. Ideal for small groups or individuals. Full board includes use of large studio and grounds (open under the National Gardens Scheme). Gourmet vegetarian food. Some painting courses available, tuition extra.
G CatB V Ve NS Acc6

# Cuffern Manor

☎ 01437 710071

## Roch, Haverfordwest, Pembrokeshire SA62 6HB

e-mail: enquiries@cuffernmanor.co.uk
website: www.cuffernmanor.co.uk

Our eighteenth-century Manor House in the spectacular Pembrokeshire countryside is adjacent to the stunning Pembrokeshire Coast National Park and 2 miles from Newgale Beach. Quality organic, fair-traded food or local produce. We specialise in serving delicious vegetarian and vegan food. Winner of Pembrokeshire Produce 2006 Award for 'Best use of local food'. See also page 11.
G INS CatB DA Ve NS CN Acc15

## *Cafés, restaurants, pubs*

**Waverley Vegetarian Restaurant** ☎ 01267 236521
   23 Lammas Street, Carmarthen, Carmarthenshire SA31 3AL

R L c w org

**The Hive on the Quay** ☎ 01545 570445
   Cadwgan Place, Aberaeron, Ceredigion SA46 0BU

C L a

**The Treehouse** ☎ 01970 615791
  14 Stryd y Popty/Baker Street, Aberystwyth, Ceredigion SY23 2BJ
  Aberystwyth's favourite café and shop for the best organic, local and
  seasonal produce. Vegans, vegetarians, carnivores and free-thinkers all
  welcome.                                                                C L a w org
**The Mulberry Bush** ☎ 01570 423317
  2 Bridge Street, Lampeter, Ceredigion SA48 7HG                C c w org
**The Refectory at St Davids**
  St Davids Cathedral, Haverfordwest, Pembrokeshire SA62 6RH    C L a

# Scotland

Orkney and Shetland
Islands (NE of the
Scottish mainland,
here shown at half
scale of main map)

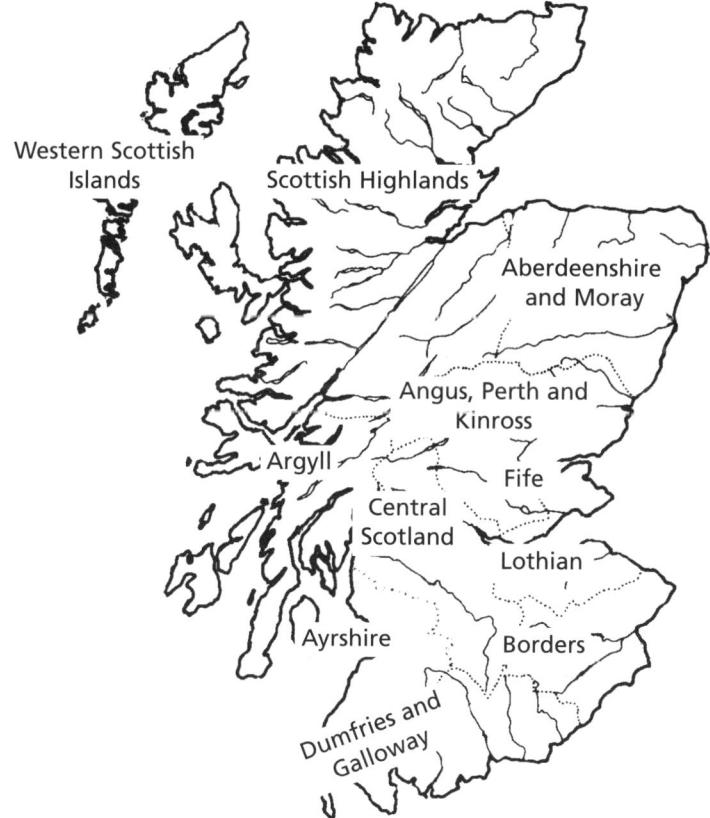

Western Scottish
Islands

Scottish Highlands

Aberdeenshire
and Moray

Angus, Perth and
Kinross

Argyll

Fife

Central
Scotland

Lothian

Ayrshire

Borders

Dumfries and
Galloway

# Aberdeenshire & Moray

## Cafés, restaurants, pubs

**The Lemon Tree Café** ☎ 01224 642694
5 West North Street, Aberdeen AB24 5AT                    C L a
**Soul and Spice Café Bar** ☎ 01224 645200
15-17 Belmont Street, Aberdeen, Aberdeenshire AB10 1JR    C L a
**Noah's Ark Bistro** ☎ 01340 821428
Fourmet House, Balvenie Street, Dufftown, Moray AB55 4AB
Excellent original vegetarian and vegan cooking in a beautiful part of
the world. We now have lovely accommodation (CatB, Acc3). Please
visit our website for latest info. www.noahsarkbistro.co.uk
R/C L a w

# Argyll

## Cafés, restaurants, pubs

**The Smiddy Bistro** ☎ 01546 603606
Smithy Lane, Lochgilphead PA31 8TA                    R L a w

# Ayrshire

## Drumskeoch Farm B&B          ☎ 01465 841172
### Pinwherry, nr Girvan KA26 0QB

e-mail: drumskeoch@wildmail.com
website: www.drumskeoch.co.uk

Unique family-run green, organic vegetarian/vegan B&B in naturally
renovated rural farmhouse, with own water source and beautiful views
of the surrounding hills. A tranquil haven with comfortable and
relaxed atmosphere, delicious food, and a great base for walking, sightseeing and relaxing. Camping also available. See also page 12.
PH INS CatB V Ve NS CN Acc4+camping

# Borders

## *Cafés, restaurants, pubs*

**Tibbie Shiels Inn** ☎ 01750 42231
St Mary's Loch, Selkirkshire, Scottish Borders TD7 5LH
This historic coaching inn is located 16 miles from Selkirk, on the
A708 to Moffat.                                                    R/P L a

# Dumfries and Galloway

## *Cafés, restaurants, pubs*

**Abbey Cottage** ☎ 01387 850377
26 Main Street, New Abbey, Dumfries DG2 8BY
Situated beside historical Sweetheart Abbey, we serve morning coffee,
light lunches and afternoon tea, baked or cooked on our premises.
Also gift shop stocking preserves and crafts from around the region.
www.abbeycottagetearoom.com

R L a w org

# Edinburgh

## Ardgarth Guest House

☎ 0131 669 3021, fax 0131 468 1221
### 3 St Mary's Place, Portobello, Edinburgh EH15 2QF

e-mail: stay@ardgarth.com
website: www.ardgarth.com

Tastefully adapted from a large
Victorian home, in a wide, quiet
street with easy parking. City centre
20 minutes by bus, short stroll to
sandy beach and a promenade that
is the envy of Edinburgh! Single,
double, twin and family rooms,
some en-suite. Cots/high chairs
available. Ground floor rooms fully equipped for disabled people.
G INS CatB DA Ve NS Acc20

# Six Mary's Place

A welcoming Georgian guest house situated in the Stockbridge area of Edinburgh – a quiet location only 10 minutes away from the city centre.
Free tea and coffee facilities and internet access, in the comfortable lounge.
Vegetarian breakfast served in a conservatory overlooking our private garden.
Opportunity to use kitchen facilities when staying in the Family Room (max 6 people sharing).

**Tel: 0131 332 8965**
**Fax: 0131 624 7060**

Six Mary's Place, Raeburn Place,
Stockbridge, Edinburgh. EH4 1JH

**www.sixmarysplace.co.uk**

*info@sixmarysplace.co.uk*

# Vegetarian Café

Voted one of Edinburgh's best vegetarian restaurants
by *List* magazine.

*Fresh home-made soup, daily selection of savouries & sweets.*

*Delicious cakes, scones, tea & coffees.*

Open Mon–Sat 10am–3.30pm

*Organic bakery & tofu products available.*

## 19 St Leonard's Lane, Edinburgh EH8 9SD

tel 0131 662 0040    admin@theengineshed.org

# Elmview

☎ 0131 228 1973

**15 Glengyle Terace, Edinburgh EH3 9LN**

e-mail: nici@elmview.co.uk
website: www.elmview.co.uk

Robin and Nici Hill's elegant and peaceful accommodation is situated in the heart of Edinburgh, only 15 minutes' walk from Princes Street and Edinburgh Castle. Totally non-smoking and graded 5 Stars by the AA.

PH INS CatA Ve NS Acc8

# Six Mary's Place Guest House

☎ 0131 332 8965, fax 0131 624 7060

**Raeburn Place, Stockbridge, Edinburgh EH4 1JH**

e-mail: info@sixmarysplace.co.uk
website: www.sixmarysplace.co.uk

See display ad on page 92.
G INS CatA Ve NS Acc23

## *Cafés, restaurants, pubs*

**The Baked Potato Shop** ☎ 0131 225 7572
    56 Cockburn Street, Edinburgh EH1 1PB
    Extensive selection of vegetarian/vegan fillings, plus vegan cakes
    home made. Open 7 days 9am-9pm.                    Take-away c
**Cornerstone Café** ☎ 0131 229 0212
    Under St John's Church, 1 Lothian Road, Edinburgh EH2 4BJ   C L a
**David Bann Restaurant** ☎ 0131 556 5888
    56-58 St Mary's Street, Edinburgh EH1 1SX                    R L c
**The Engine Shed** ☎ 0131 662 0040
    19 St Leonard's Lane, Edinburgh EH8 9SD
    See display ad on page 92.                              R/C c org
**Filmhouse Café Bar** ☎ 0131 229 5932
    88 Lothian Road, Edinburgh EH3 9BZ                      C L a org

**Henderson's Bistro** ☎ 0131 225 2605
25 Thistle Street, Edinburgh EH2 1DR                         R L c w org
**Henderson's Salad Table** ☎ 0131 225 2131
94 Hanover Street, Edinburgh EH2 1DR
See display ad above.                                        R L c w org
**Henderson's Wine Bar** ☎ 0131 225 2131
94 Hanover Street, Edinburgh EH2 1DR           Wine bar L c w org
**Kalpna Restaurant** ☎ 0131 667 9890
2-3 St Patrick Square, Edinburgh EH8 9EZ                     R L c w

## Adelaide's

☎ 0141 248 4970, fax 0141 226 4247

### 209 Bath Street, Glasgow G2 4HZ

e-mail: reservations@adelaides.co.uk
website: www.adelaides.co.uk

Highly acclaimed Guest House situated in award-winning listed building with family/twin/double and single en-suites available. Our friendly, knowledgeable staff make Adelaide's *the* ideal base from which to explore Glasgow, The Friendly City.

G INS CatA Ve NS Acc20

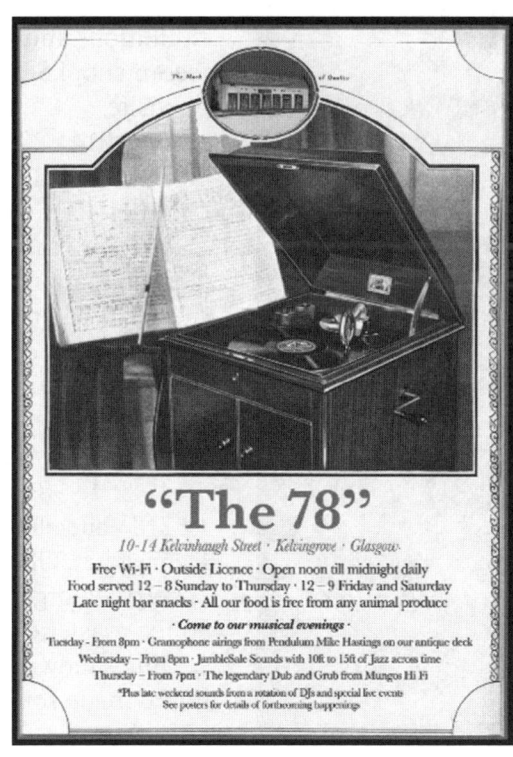

## Cafés, restaurants, pubs

**Grassroots Café** ☎0141 333 0534
93-97 St George's Road,
Charing Cross, Glasgow G3 6JA
Innovative vegetarian and
vegan food served in laid-back
Bohemian surroundings.
Freshly baked organic cakes
and delicious organic coffee.
Open 7 days a week.
R/C L c w org

**mono** ☎ 0141 553 2400
12 Kings Court, King Street,
Glasgow G1 5RB
Exciting café/bar in Glasgow's
Merchant City. Great range of
tasty animal-free dishes.
Including grocery, library,
exhibitions and fantastic
record shop! See display ad
opposite.          C/P L d w org

**stereo** ☎ 0141 222 2254
20-28 Renfield Lane, Glasgow
G2 6PH
City Centre café/bar near
Central Station. Breads, pies,
cakes baked on premises.
Healthy sit-in or take-away.
Great salads and coffee.
C/P L d w org

**Tapa Coffee & Bakehouse**
☎ 0141 554 9981
19-21 Whitehill Street,
Dennistoun, Glasgow G31 2LH
A certified organic bakery,
coffee roasterie and café
serving sandwiches, foccacia,
home-made soups, salads and

delicious cakes. Served with freshly roasted coffee.        C c w org

**The 78** ☎ 0141 576 5018
14 Kelvinhaugh Street, Glasgow G3 8NU
Delightful pub in west end of Glasgow serving delicious and healthy
animal-free food. Organic drinks, real fire, 1927 gramophone! See
display ad on page 95.                    P L d w org

# *The Scottish Highlands*

## The Inn                          ☎ 01520 522257
### Dalwhinnie, Inverness-shire PH19 1AG

e-mail: sarah@theinndalwhinnie.com
website: www.theinndalwhinnie.com

Enjoy creative vegetarian cuisine at
the coolest hotel in the Highlands.
Think fresh, local ingredients, free
trade organic coffee, big fat sofas,
lounge music and complimentary wi-
fi. Our specials boards are ever
changing to encompass the finest
seasonal produce on offer.
H CatB L DA Ve NS Acc49

## Cuildorag House                   ☎ 01855 821529
### Onich, nr Fort William, Inverness-shire PH33 6SD

e-mail: enquiries@cuildoraghouse.com
website: www.cuildoraghouse.com

Stay and relax in our comfortable
Victorian house set amongst
spectacular lochs and mountains. Large
delicious breakfasts and evening meals
(often organic and from the garden).
Days walking, mountain biking,
touring, exploring Ben Nevis, Glencoe,
Ardnamurchan, castles, steam trains …
PH CatB V Ve NS Acc6

# Woodland

☎ 01549 441715

## Rosehall, by Lairg, Sutherland IV27 4BD

e-mail: mail@vegetarian-scotland.com
website: www.vegetarian-scotland.com

Woodland is a Vegan and Vegetarian B&B. Vegan evening meals can be supplied by arrangement. Woodland is the ideal place to explore the Scottish Highlands, being centrally placed. There are good walks locally and plenty of wildlife. Yoga retreats also offered, please see www.yogaretreatuk.co.uk. See also page 12.

PH INS CatB DA V Ve NS CN Acc6

---

# Foxwood

Foxwood is surrounded by inspirational countryside, standing in 4 acres of land with sea and mountain views. The sunrises and sunsets can be unbelievable.

*Spacious en-suites, and single room.*

*Sauna, jacuzzi, steam cabinet and alternative therapies are available.*

*Ideal for touring, walking, cycling, relaxing.*

## 11a Ullinish by Struan, Isle of Skye IV56 8FD

e-mail treefox@hotmail.com
website www.scotland–info.co.uk/foxwood

---

## Cafés, restaurants, pubs

**Cawdor Castle** ☎ 01667 404401
Nairn, Inverness-shire IV12 5RD
R L a org (open 1st May to 2nd Sunday in October)
**Station Tea Room and Craft Shop** ☎ 01349 865894
Station Square, Dingwall, Ross-shire IV15 9NW         C a
**Plockton Seafood Restaurant** ☎ 01599 544423
Railway Building, Plockton, Ross-shire IV52 8TT     R L a org
**The Ceilidh Place** ☎ 01854 612103
West Argyle Street, Ullapool, Ross-shire IV26 2TY    R/C/P L a org
**Loch Croispol Bookshop, Restaurant & Gallery** ☎ 01971 511777
2 Balnakeil Craft Village, Durness, by Lairg, Sutherland IV27 4PT
R L a

# Shetland Islands

## Cafés, restaurants, pubs

**Da Böd Café** ☎ 01806 503348
Hillswick Wildlife Sanctuary, Hillswick ZE2 9RW
We serve vegetarian and vegan food in a 400-
year-old building. Open May to September
from 11am, please phone to book an evening
meal. Payment by donation. Also B&B for 2
people in a lovely room with sea views. All
proceeds go to Hillswick Wildlife Sanctuary,
a seal and otter sanctuary.     C c w org

# The Western Scottish Islands

## Foxwood       ☎ 01470 572331

### 11A Ullinish by Struan, Isle of Skye IV56 8FD

e-mail: treefox@hotmail.com
website: www.scotland-info.co.uk/foxwood

See display ad on page 98.
G CatB DA V Ve NS CN Acc6

## *Cafés, restaurants, pubs*

**An Tuireann Arts Centre and Café** ☎ 01478 613306
  Struan Road, Portree, Isle of Skye IV51 9EG
  See display ad above.                                      C L a
**JJ's Bistro** ☎ 01470 572782
  Struan, Isle of Skye IV56 8FB                         R L a org

# Further vegetarian information

For users of this guide who would like further information on vegetarianism or veganism in Britain, or information on a particular area, we list below a number of organisations, groups and information centres. When writing, please include a stamp for return postage.

## National

Friends Vegetarian Society
  9 Astons Close, Woods Lane, Amblecote, nr Stourbridge, West Midlands DY5 2QT, tel 01384 423899
Jewish Vegetarian Society
  855 Finchley Road, London NW11 8LX, tel 020 8455 0692
Muslim Vegan/Vegetarian Society
  59 Bray Towers, 136 Adelaide Road, London NW3 3JU, tel 020 7483 1742
  Run by Rafeeque Ahmed, who has written a booklet called 'Islam and Vegetarianism' which is available at £1.
The Vegetarian Society (UK) Ltd.
  Parkdale, Dunham Road, Altrincham, Cheshire WA14 4QG, tel 0161 925 2000, fax 0161 926 9182
The Vegan Society Ltd.
  21 Hylton Street, Hockley, Birmingham B18 6HJ, tel 0845 458 8244/0121 523 1730
Viva! (Vegetarians International Voice for Animals)
  8 York Court, Wilder Street, Bristol BS2 8QH, tel 0845 456 8220, fax 0845 456 8230

Viva! actively and successfully campaigns to stop cruelty to animals and to promote a vegetarian/vegan lifestyle. Free information available from the above address.
Young Indian Vegetarians
  226 London Road, West Croydon, Surrey CR0 2TF, e-mail animalahimsa@yahoo.co.uk

## England (by county)

Bedfordshire Vegetarians
  The Old Spinney, 69 The Ridgeway, Flitwick, Bedfordshire MK45 1DJ, e-mail bunnymunch@hotmail.com
Bedford Veggies & Vegans
  Tel 01234 741253, e-mail greenkatgreen@hotmail.co.uk
Thames Valley Vegans & Vegetarians
  68 Peppard Road, Emmer Green, Reading, Berkshire RG4 8TL, tel 0118 946 4858, e-mail t3v@makessense.co.uk
Chiltern Veggies
  7 Bedford Avenue, Amersham, Buckinghamshire HP6 6PT, tel 01753 893069, e-mail chilternveggies@yahoo.co.uk

Milton Keynes Vegetarians & Vegans
13 Peers Lane, Shenley Church
End, Milton Keynes,
Buckinghamshire MK5 6BG, tel
01908 503919, e-mail
mkvegan475@fsmail.net

Peterborough Vegetarian Society
28 Glendale, Orton Wistow,
Peterborough, Cambridgeshire
PE2 6YL, tel 01733 230314, e-
mail pboroveggies@hotmail.co.uk

Chester & Clwyd Vegetarians
Nant Yr Hafod Cottage, Hafod
Bilston, Llandegla, Clwyd LL11
3BG, tel 01978 790442, e-mail
indesigneko@aol.com

Tees Valley Veggies & Vegans
3 Church Lane, Marske by the
Sea, Redcar TS11 7LJ, tel 07950
017928, e-mail
tees_veg@yahoo.co.uk

Newquay Info Centre (Cornwall)
tel 01637 876987, e-mail
katie@wise.myzen.co.uk

North Cornwall Vegetarian
Information Centre
Hilltop Animal Haven, Thurdon,
Kilkhampton, Bude, Cornwall
EX23 9RZ, tel 01288 321268, e-
mail
charlesandgillian@hilltophaven.fs
net.co.uk

Right Life Information Centre
49 Upper Chapel, Launceston,
Cornwall PL15 7DW, tel 01566
776256, e-mail
rightlife.vic@btinternet.com

Lakeland Living Veg Group
15 Challoner Street,
Cockermouth, Cumbria CA13
9QS, tel 01900 824045, e-mail

veggielakelandliving@tiscali.co.uk

Amber Valley Vegetarians & Vegans
(Derbyshire)
Tel 01773 833294, e-mail
amberveg@hotmail.co.uk

Derby Vegetarian Society
P.O. Box 41, Derby DE1 9ZR, tel
0870 027 3654, e-mail
manjit01@ntlworld.com

Derbyshire Vegetarians
tel 01298 72472

Dartveggie (Dartmouth, Devon, area)
e-mail dartveggie@hotmail.co.uk

North & Mid Devon Vegetarian Info
Centre
Fern Tor, Meshaw, South Molton,
Devon EX36 4NA, tel 01769
550339, e-mail veg@ferntor.co.uk

Plymouth Environment Centre
11a Fredington Grove,
Milehouse, Plymouth, Devon
PL2 3EA, tel 01752 564434, e-
mail deaconeig@aol.com

Bournemouth Vegetarian Society
Flat A15, 20 Dean Park Road,
Bournemouth, Dorset BH1 1JB,
tel 01202 555712

Barking Vegetarian Info Centre
288 Howard Road, Barking,
Essex IG11 7DN, tel 020 8252
5846 evenings

North Essex Vegetarian Information
tel 01206 263545, e-mail
APWh@aol.com

Southend Animal Aid
PO Box 211, Short Street,
Southend on Sea, Essex SS1
1AA, tel 01268 756026, e-mail
southendanimalaid@hotmail.com

Southend Area Veggies Information
Centre (Essex)
tel 01702 540903, e-mail
soocoleman4@aol.com
Vegan Harlow Info Centre (Essex)
tel 07754 166813, e-mail
info@veganharlow.co.uk
VegSX
4 Tyrrells Road, Billericay, Essex
CM11 2QE, tel 07970 732668, e-
mail veganessex@hotmail.com
Manchester Vegetarian & Vegan
Group
550 St Helens Road, Bolton BL3
3SJ, tel 01204 654401, e-mail
mike@mvvg.co.uk
Vegetarian Information
100 Sarah Robinson House,
Queen Street, Portsmouth,
Hampshire PO1 3JA, tel 023
9275 3956
Solent Vegetarians & Vegans
(Hampshire)
tel 023 8064 3813, e-mail
info@solentveg.org.uk
Wye Valley Veggies
6 Bearcroft, Weobley, Hereford
HR4 8TA, tel 01432 277493, e-
mail info@w-v-v.org.uk
Isle of Wight Vegetarians
Keepers Lock, Youngwood Way,
Alverstone Garden Village,
Sandown, Isle of Wight PO36
0HF, tel 01983 407098, e-mail
johnvl@tiscali.co.uk
Bexleyheath & Erith Vegetarian Info
Centre (Kent)
tel 01322 402713, mobile 07986
670470
Broadstairs Veggie Info Centre
11 Queens Road, Broadstairs,

Kent CT10 1NU, tel 01843
601247, e-mail
copperfieldsbb@btinternet.com
Bromley Eating Experience
241 Pickhurst Rise, West
Wickham, Kent BR4 0AH, tel
020 8777 1680
Canterbury & Coastal Information
Centre
83 Cherry Gardens, Herne Bay,
Kent CT6 5QY, tel 01227 375661
Medway Veggies & Vegans
7 Masefield Drive, Cliffe Woods,
Rochester, Kent ME3 8JW, tel
01634 294865, e-mail
sheilamccrossan@hotmal.com
North Kent Vegetarian Info Centre
Sycamore Lodge, 71 Barton Hill
Drive, Minster on Sea, Sheerness,
Kent ME12 3NF, tel 01795
873987
Sevenoaks Vegetarians, Vegans and
Fellow Travellers
Westmount, Orchard Road,
Pratts Bottom, Orpington, Kent
BR6 7NT, tel 01689 859716, e-
mail
iangallehawk@blueyonder.co.uk
Tunbridge Wells Vegan & Vegetarian
Group (Kent)
The Little Barn, Puxtye Farm,
Crouch Lane, Sandhurst, Kent
TN18 5PB, tel 01580 850631, e-
mail mark.hanna@virgin.net
Natural Healing
Elaine Aspin, 86 Queen Street,
Great Harwood, Lancashire BB6
7AL, tel 01254 882233 (info
centre in a holistic treatment
centre)

Lancs Veg
tel 01772 787163, mobile 07866 788580, e-mail jj.dave@virgin.net

Wellbeing Workshops Veg Info Centre
Green Cottage, 514 Halliwell Road, St Paul's Conservation, Bolton, Lancashire BL1 8BP, tel 07050 256916, e-mail alwynne@wellbeingworkshopswo rldwide.com

Leicestershire Vegetarian and Vegan Group
Beeches, Smeeton Road, Saddington, Leicestershire LE8 0QT, tel 07786 175445, e-mail leicesterveggies@isd.co.uk

Grimsby Vegetarians
Flat 3, 6 Regent Gardens, Grimsby, Lincolnshire DN34 5AT, tel 01472 870738, e-mail grimsby.vegetarians@tesco.net

Lincoln Vegetarians & Vegans Info Centre
tel 01522 576441, e-mail ros.7spireview@virgin.net

Louth Vegetarian Group (Lincolnshire)
37 Church Lane, Manby, Lincolnshire LN11 8HL, tel 01507 327687

Lesbian Vegans (London)
tel 020 7243 8225, e-mail tiger@tiger3.plus.com

South West London Veg Group
Flat 424, Brandenburgh House, 116 Fulham Palace Road, London W6 9HH, tel 020 8741 6793, e-mail swveg1@yahoo.co.uk

Merseyside Vegetarian Helplink
38 Hyacinth Close, Haydock, St Helens, Merseyside WA11 0NZ, tel 01942 271761, e-mail marg4646@hotmail.com

ScouseVeg
tel 0151 933 1338, e-mail jane@vegsoc.org

Harrow Vegetarian Society
152 Kenton Road, Harrow, Middlesex HA3 8AZ, tel 020 8907 1235, e-mail kjoshi@pradipsweet.co.uk

Norfolk Vegetarian & Vegan Society
13 Ipswich Grove, Norwich, Norfolk NR2 2LU, tel 01603 620784, e-mail aliciahowell@hotmail.co.uk

Northants Veggies
106 Eastfield Road, Wellingborough, Northamptonshire NN8 1PA, tel 01933 381731, e-mail jane.mills7@ntlworld.com

Wellingborough Information Centre
Fieldview, 54 Grange Road, Redhill Grange, Wellingborough, Northamptonshire NN9 5YQ, tel 01933 674311, e-mail linda.burton@54grange.co.uk

Nottingham Vegetarian & Vegan Society
245 Gladstone Street, Nottingham NG7 6HX, tel 0845 458 9595, e-mail nvvs@veggies.org.uk

Oxford Vegetarians
57 Sharland Close, Grove, Wantage, Oxfordshire OX12 0AF, tel 01235 769425, e-mail oxfordveg@ivu.org

Oswestry Vegetarian Information Centre
Hobnob House, Maesbury Marsh, Oswestry, Shropshire SY10 8JH, tel 01691 670404, webmaster@ivu.org

Shropshire Veggies & Vegans
1 Lees Farm Drive, Madeley, Telford, Shropshire TF7 5SU, tel 01952 588878, e-mail david.whalley@talk21.com

North Somerset Vegetarian & Vegan Info Centre
tel 01934 843853, e-mail rogerhards@venusmead.go-plus.net

4 Paws 1 Planet Animal Welfare & Environmental Information Centre
Freshfields, School Bank, Hollington, Stoke-on-Trent, Staffordshire ST10 4HH, tel 01889 507274, e-mail hilarydp@gotadsl.co.uk

Lichfield District Vegetarian Info Centre
29 Spring Road, Lichfield, Staffordshire WS13 6BJ, tel 07852 190855, e-mail lichfield@veggiefriends.com

Animals in Need (Woking)
7 Candlerush Close, Maybury, Woking, Surrey GU22 8AT, tel 01483 871392, e-mail david.rainford4@ntlworld.com

Croydon Vegetarian Group
Flat 23, Zodiac Court, 165 London Road, Croydon, Surrey CR0 2RJ, tel 020 8688 6325

Guildford Vegetarian Society (Surrey)
Tel 01483 425040

Kingston & Richmond Vegetarians
87 Porchester Road, Kingston-upon-Thames, Surrey KT1 3PW, tel 020 8541 3437, e-mail martin.h2o@tiscali.co.uk

Twickenham & Surrey Vegetarian & Vegan Group
tel 01372 884368, e-mail twsurreyveg@mailbolt.com

Woking Veggie & Vegan Group (Surrey)
wokingveg@aol.com

Arun Vegetarian Info Centre (Sussex)
tel 01903 775236, e-mail jvandepoll@aol.com

Lewes & Hastings Area Vegetarian & Vegan Group
Sandhills Oast, Bodle Street, nr Hailsham, East Sussex BN27 4QU, tel 01435 830150, e-mail JLJDRJ@aol.com

VegNE
1 Poplar Place, Gosforth, Newcastle upon Tyne, Tyne & Wear NE3 1DR, tel 0191 285 9980, e-mail mike@casselden.unisonplus.net

Coventry Vegetarians & Vegans (Warwickshire)
tel 024 7663 4115, e-mail cov.veggies@hotmail.com

Birmingham Vegetarians & Vegans
54-57 Allison Street, Digbeth, Birmingham, West Midlands B5 5TH, tel 0121 353 2442, e-mail info@bvv.org.uk

Wolverhampton Veggies & Vegans
73 Oak Street, Merridale, Wolverhampton, West Midlands WV3 0AH, tel 01902 682550, e-mail wolvesveggies@yahoo.co.uk

Swindon Veggies & Animal Concern
(Wiltshire)
tel 01793 644796, e-mail
denisvegan01@tiscali.co.uk
Redditch Vegetarians & Vegans
PO Box 10202, Redditch,
Worcestershire B98 8YT, tel
01527 458395, e-mail
reddiveggie@lycos.com
Bradford Vegetarian Society
66 Kirkgate, Shipley, West
Yorkshire BD18 3EL, tel 01274
598455, e-mail
atmatrasi@btinternet.com
The Green House Info Centre
5 Station Parade, Harrogate,
North Yorkshire HG1 1UF, tel
01423 502580
Leeds Vegetarian Society (West
Yorkshire)
tel 0113 248 4044, e-mail
natalie@tharraleos.freeserve.co.uk
North Riding Vegetarians & Vegans
Cottage no 3, Arrathorne, Bedale,
North Yorkshire DL8 1NA, tel
0845 458 4714, e-mail
patricia@p-m-t.freeserve.co.uk
Sheffield & District (South Yorkshire)
e-mail cheznous.post@virgin.net
South Yorkshire Vegetarian Group
e-mail mymitzi@lycos.co.uk

# Scotland

Aberdeen Vegetarian Information
Centre
17 Howburn Place, Aberdeen
AB11 6XT, tel 01224 573034, e-
mail
george_rodger1940@yahoo.co.uk
Clyde Coast (South) Information
Centre
Old Sawmill Cottage, Kilkerran,
Maybole KA19 7PZ, tel 01655
740451, e-mail
kilkerran@breathemail.net
Glasgow & District Vegetarian
Information Centre
66 Bellahouston Drive, Glasgow
G52 1HQ, tel 0141 882 5650
(evenings), e-mail
gedandmary@hotmail.com
Highland Veggies & Vegans
tel 01997 421109, e-mail
info@highlandveggies.org
Morayshire Vegetarian & Vegan
Group
Hamewith, Mount Street,
Dufftown, Keith, Banffshire
AB55 4FH, tel 01340 820292, e-
mail ughamewith@aol.com
South East Scotland Vegetarians
2 New Woodside, Bush Estate,
Penicuik, Midlothian EH26 0PH,
tel 0131 445 1714, e-mail
sesv@ivu.org
Scottish Borders Vegetarian
Information Centre
131 Roxburgh Street, Kelso TD5
7DU, tel 01573 225793, e-mail
stuart.heritage@breathemail.net
Tay Veggies
10 Hillpark Road, Wormit,

Newport on Tay, Fife DD6 8PR,
tel 01382 541140, e-mail
tayveggies@gmail.com

## Wales

Bridgend Vegetarian Information
  Centre
  2 Fairways, North Cornelly,
  Bridgend, Glamorgan CF33
  4DH, tel 01656 742008, e-mail
  bryn.mor@hotmail.co.uk
Caldicot Vegetarian Info Centre
  30 Westway, Rogiet, Caldicot,
  South Wales NP26 3SP, tel 01291
  424362, e-mail
  texas.veggie@clara.co.uk
Cardiff and the Vale Vegetarian
  Group
  19 Pomeroy Street, Cardiff CF10
  5GS, tel 07790 742868, e-mail
  cardiff-vale-
  vegetarians@hotmail.co.uk
Chester & Clwyd Vegetarians
  Nant Yr Hafod Cottage, Hafod
  Bilston, Llandegla, Clwyd LL11
  3BG, tel 01978 790442, e-mail
  indesigneko@aol.com
Powys Vegetarian Info Centre
  20 Ffordd Mynydd Griffiths,
  Machynlleth, Powys SY20 8DD,
  tel 01654 702562
South West Wales Vegetarian Group
  Glanrhydw Cottage, Cloigyn,
  Pontantwn, Kidwelly,
  Carmarthenshire SA17 5NB, tel
  01267 232733, e-mail
  grahamesme.goddard@btinternet.
  com

# VisitBritain offices

Overseas readers: your nearest VisitBritain (previously the British Tourist Authority) office will be pleased to provide you with maps, guides and travel advice. General information as well as the offices' e-mail and website addresses can be found at www.visitbritain.com while the Britain and London Visitor Centre, 1 Regent Street, London SW1Y 4XT can help with travel information once you have arrived in this country.

AUSTRALIA
> VisitBritain, Level 2, 15 Blue Street, North Sydney, NSW 2060

AUSTRIA
> Britain Visitor Centre, c/o The British Council, Siebensterngasse 21, 1070 Wien

BELGIUM
> Visit Britain, BP 25, 1040 Etterbeek 2

BRAZIL
> Turismo Britanico - VisitBritain, Centro Brasileiro Britanico, Rua Ferreira de Araujo 741, 1 andar, Pinheiros, Sao Paulo, SP 05428-002

CANADA
> VisitBritain, 5915 Airport Road, Suite 120, Mississauga, Ontario L4V 1T1

CHINA
> VisitBritain, c/o Cultural and Education Section British Embassy, 4/F Landmark Building Tower 1, 8 North Dongsanhuan Road, Chaoyang District, 100004 Beijing
> VisitBritain, c/o British Consulate General Shanghai, 1st Floor Cross Tower, 318 Fu Zhou Lu, 200001 Shanghai

DENMARK
> VisitBritain, Kristianiagade 8, 3., 2100 København

FRANCE
> VisitBritain, 22 Avenue Franklin Roosevelt, 75008 Paris

GERMANY
> VisitBritain & Britain Visitor Centre, Dorotheenstrasse 54, 10117 Berlin

GREECE
> VisitBritain, 29 Michalakopoulou Street, Athens 11528

HONG KONG
> 7/F VisitBritain, The British Council, 3 Supreme Court Road, Admiralty

HUNGARY
> VisitBritain, 1063 Budapest, Bajnok u. 19

INDIA
> VisitBritain, 202-203 JMD Regent Square, 2nd Floor, Mehrauli Gurgaon Road, Gurgaon, Haryana – 122 001
> VisitBritain, c/o British Council Division, British Deputy High Commission, Mittal Tower 'C' Wing, 2nd Floor, Nariman Point, Mumbai 400 021
> VisitBritain, c/o Ms. Advisers, No. 489, 2nd Floor, 10th Main, 8th Cross, Jeevan Bhima Nagar Main Road, HAL 3rd Stage, Bangalore – 560 075

**ITALY**

Ente Nazionale Britannico per il Turismo, Via Cesare Cantù 3, 20123 Milano

**JAPAN**

VisitBritain, Akasaka Twin Tower 1F, 2-17-22 Akasaka, Minato-ku, Tokyo 107-0052

**MALAYSIA**

VisitBritain, c/o The British Council, Ground Floor, West Block, Wisma Selangor Dredging, 142C Jalan Ampang, 50450 Kuala Lumpur

**NETHERLANDS**

VisitBritain, Prins Hendrikkade 186-187, 1011 TD Amsterdam. Post: Postbus 20650, 1001 NR Amsterdam

**NEW ZEALAND**

VisitBritain, c/o British Consulate-General Office, Level 17, IAG House, 151 Queen Street, PO Box 105-652, Auckland

**NORWAY**

Det Britiske Turistkontor, Olav V's gate 5, 0161 Oslo. Post: PB 1554 Vika, 0117 Oslo

**PORTUGAL**

VisitBritain Portugal, Largo Rafael Bordalo Pinheiro 16, 2o piso, sala 210, 1200-396 Lisboa

**RUSSIA**

VisitBritain, c/o The British Council, VGBIL, Nikoloyamskaya 1, Moscow 109189

**SINGAPORE**

VisitBritain, 600 North Bridge Road, #09-10 Parkview Square, 188778

**SOUTH AFRICA**

VisitBritain, Lancaster Gate, Hyde Park Lane, Hyde Park, Sandton 2196

**SOUTH KOREA**

VisitBritain, c/o British Embassy, Taepyeongno 40, 4 Jeong-dong, Jung-gu, Seoul (100-120)

**SPAIN**

Turismo Británico, C/ Caidos de la Division Azul 20, 28016 Madrid. Post: Apartado de Correos 19205, 28080 Madrid

**SWEDEN**

Brittiska Turistbyrån, Klara Norra Kyrkogata 29, 111 22 Stockholm. Post: Box 3102, 103 62 Stockholm

**THAILAND**

VisitBritain, c/o The British Council, 254 Chulalongkorn Soi 64 Siam Square, Phyathai Road Pathumwan, Bangkok 10330

**UNITED ARAB EMIRATES**

VisitBritain, 2nd Floor, Sharaf Building, Khalid Bin Waleed Road, Dubai. Post: PO Box 33342, Dubai

**USA**

VisitBritain, 551 Fifth Avenue, Suite 701, New York NY 10176-0799

VisitBritain, 625 N. Michigan Avenue, Suite 1001, Chicago IL 60611-1977

VisitBritain, 10880 Wilshire Blvd, Suite 570, Los Angeles CA 90024